Breaking The Cycle of Self-Abuse

Lucreta Bowman

With
Sadell Bradley

Forward By
Bishop Michael Dantley

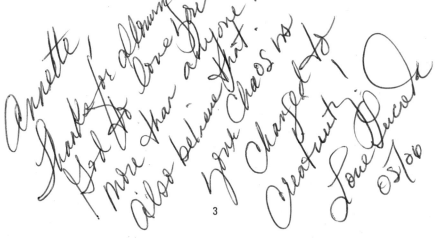

Lucreta Bowman
1947 Auburn Avenue
Cincinnati, OH 45219
513-345-1082
lbowman@citygospelmission.com

Cover and book design by Laura Brown
Cover photo of Lucreta by C. Smith

All proceeds from the sale of this book will be directed to:
City Gospel Mission
Cincinnati, Ohio

Breaking The Cycle of Self-Abuse

"Breaking the Cycle of Self-Abuse" is both sobering and uplifting at the same time. I was struck by what must have been a difficult look back at your life experience. The book is insightful about your recovery as well as your giving back to the community with the *Having The Courage To Change* program. Clearly, your story, which you talk about at length in the book, should be inspiring to all who read it. I know that you have been through many trials and tribulations in your life, but it is a joy to see your success and to read your story. Talbert House is pleased to play a small part in your recovery.

Neil F. Tilow, President, Talbert House

It has been a blessing to watch Lucreta mature into a strong, leading woman of faith. Knowing that it would require rapid growth to lead others from the prison of an incarcerated mind, Lucreta sought out and submitted to the mentoring process in her own life. Her submission to our leadership has brought her tremendous reward as she has become a sought-after leader herself. It has been my privilege to serve her and the ministry of *Having The Courage To Change.*

Deborah Merritt, Executive Pastor
Christ Emmanuel Christian Fellowship

When my wife and I started *Having The Courage To Change* I didn't know how much God would use the ministry to impact not only other's lives, but most of all our own. It has been a wonderful journey and I'm looking forward to more adventures with the love of my life.

Charles Bowman

Table of Contents

Dedication

I dedicate this book, which is "His story" of my life, to the
greatest chess player I have ever met: God The Father, Jesus
The Son, and The Holy Spirit. Thank You for taking my life and
creating the opportunity for me to believe that not only was change
possible, but that I could experience it and possess it.

I also dedicate this book to all those who desire change and have
found themselves uncomfortable in their present condition.

Acknowledgements

I would like to thank the Lord my God for coming after me when I had lost all direction and hope. I also want to say how much I appreciate my husband, Charles Bowman, and my son, Kimm DeLorean Hamilton, for just loving me. Sadell M. Bradley, I am grateful you allowed God to release your gift of creativity in this book. Pam Washington, I am blessed because you are such a servant; you remind me of an Aaron because you are always there holding up my arms to bring forth my vision in excellence. Bishop Dantley, Pastor Carol, Elder Merritt, and all the leadership at Christ Emmanuel Christian Fellowship, thanks for teaching me how to fly in the Gospel of Christ. Roger Howell and Ed Perrine, thanks for allowing me to teach others how to fly and land in this life through the holistic approach to making disciples. Thanks to my friends who pray with me and for me, especially my Monday night Covenant Group. Also thanks to my Staff and Partners in the Ministry. I especially want to say thanks to the Participants of *Having the Courage to Change* Ministry — the past ones, present ones, and those who have yet to come — for trusting the God in me. I want to also thank those God used to help me through my journey of change, especially Mary Helen Williams, my mother, who taught me what love is in action, and to my entire family - the one God chose for me. I am also grateful to the process called Change...

Lucreta Bowman

Life Lesson

When the student is taking the test the teacher doesn't teach,
Because the teacher knows you have been prepared for the test,
And what you need to pass the test is already inside of you -
When faith in God graduates, it turns to trust in God,
regardless of our present situation.

One of my greatest lessons was to learn that God uses people to
teach us what *He* wants us to know about life and ourselves. In
my journey I met a man named Maurice McCrackin, better known
as Mac, who encouraged me to be and do what the Lord had
created me to become. His words to me were these,
"Some people teach others to fly, but God gave you the gift of
teaching them to fly *and land*. Now go and teach them"

Thanks Mac.

Preface

Several years ago an enthusiastic young woman whom I really did not know at the time, ran up to me and exclaimed, *"You and I are going to work together!"* with a surety that I found somewhat alarming. I replied, "Let's wait and see what develops." I believe in allowing relationships to flow, and not to be forced. Later, she showed me a manuscript of her first attempt at writing her own life story.

I had heard '*Lucretia*' Bowman speak in church. I admired her forthrightness and willingness to expose her wounds and sordid past for the sake of freeing herself and others. The atmosphere in the room was filled with a power like electric current as she boldly declared her new convictions, and her decision to change her life for good. I had hope after hearing her story, that anyone could be healed and set free from their hurtful patterns and bondage, no matter how dark.

Over time, our friendship, life experience, and maturity level grew. It was several years after that first encounter that she approached me again, asking for a "speaking coach," and for me to write the story of her life and the program she had founded, *Having the Courage to Change.* We began to hold coaching sessions and do homework. By now, Lucreta had been asked to speak and consult at prisons, churches, halfway houses, and even on local and national media. She was as determined about improving her speaking as she had been about changing her life.

Over the last three years we traveled the journey of writing *Breaking the Cycle of Self-Abuse.* I would sit and interview Lucreta, asking probing questions that would sometimes lead her to describe memories and feelings that evoked tears of joy, pain and thanksgiving. I believe she began to realize at each session how far she had come, and how blessed she was to discover that she could begin to value herself and enjoy a quality of life despite the things that had happened to her over the years. It was empowering for all of us, as we hope this book will be for you.

I would return to my computer after each meeting and endeavor to capture the sentiment, style and power of her experience in written words with metaphors and anecdotes to create pictures in the reader's imagination. I believe that the words, images and spirit of this book will assist you in seeing yourself recover and change your life completely, no matter your station in life.

If you desire to break the cycle of abuse, this book is definitely for you. If you are currently working with or serving the abused, wounded, imprisoned (physically, mentally, emotionally, or spiritually), this book will assist you. *If you are a skeptic about whether or not you or a person you love is beyond help, don't give up on them or yourself until you've read this book!*

It has been an honor for me to be a part of this project, and to be a friend to Lucreta Bowman. Lucreta has changed *her* life. This book will inspire and challenge *YOU* to have the courage to change *YOURS!* Abusive cycles can be broken, begin *TODAY* and free yourself forever!

M. Sadell Bradley

Forward

B reaking *The Cycle of Self-Abuse* is a powerful demonstration of the restorative work of God in lives of people willing to reflect and go through the arduous work of reform and reconstruction. In this compelling book, Lucreta Bowman has taken exceptionally bold steps to use her own self-disclosure to assist others in having the courage to change.

There is a liberating poignancy in Lucreta's handling of the issue of self-abuse. The traditional way of perceiving the misfortunes of our lives is to couch them in the episodes of external abuse or other instances where people and circumstances have negatively impacted our lives. For years, psychologists and counselors have sought to liberate and console us through placing blame for our less-than-stellar lives on the impact and influence of others - especially those in authority in our lives. While *Breaking The Cycle of Self-Abuse* acknowledges this phenomenon, Lucreta moves this notion even further by arguing that it is in the acceptance and even the celebration of this external abuse that we then embrace ourselves as victims and continue the abuse through self-infliction. We develop patterns of behavior to assuage the pain of external abuse that are grounded in unhealthy and self-deprecating ways. So essentially, long after the external abuse has stopped, the self-abuse replaces it and holds us prisoner to our own thinking and perceptions about ourselves. This is a terribly difficult phenomenon to fathom, but Lucreta does a great job, especially through her disclosure of her own personal journey, to get the readers to engage the possibilities of their own self-abuse and the need to end that cycle.

When one reads Lucreta's personal journey, it is so clear that only the Lord could have orchestrated her restoration and reconstruction. When she heard the words of the still, small voice, *"You will never have definition and meaning until you come back to the source,"* the beginning of her reconstruction was taking shape.

In her book, Lucreta clearly demonstrates that going through abuse to ultimate victory can be a long and circuitous process but it is underpinned by the words of Jeremiah 29:11 where the Lord's intention is to bring us to an expected end, one with a hope and a future. There are no magic tricks in this book. There are no instances of "abracadabra" and "poof" everything is miraculously better. Indeed, *Breaking The Cycle of Self-Abuse* causes readers to know clearly that perseverance and genuine struggle are essential elements to ultimate victory.

Through this book, we are forced to come face-to-face with the idea that so often our infirmities, weaknesses, or those unhealthy aspects of our personalities, and indeed, our lives become our oldest and dearest friends. When the old and familiar are given the liberty to contour our responses, life patterns and behaviors, then we perpetuate this cycle of self-abuse and learn to adapt, welcome and celebrate it. Fortunately, through the application sections at the end of each chapter, readers are compelled to personally and critically reflect and to think deeply about experiences as well as mental models that perpetuate our unhealthy, self-abusing behaviors.

While this book is challenging and hard-hitting emotionally, it offers practical solutions to readers who are committed to change. Section Two of the book provides pragmatic ways for the reader to deal with the kinds of personal changes that demand prayer, perseverance and persistence. The initial step to reconstruction and probably the hardest to personally embrace is what Lucreta calls "coming to the end of yourself and surrendering to God."

Breaking the Cycle of Self-Abuse draws the readers into themselves and then directs them to a life with others free of unhealthy perceptions and behaviors. It places the work of the Lord in a very practical context and gives readers hope and practical tools to live restored lives.

I commend Lucreta for this bold venture. Many will be not only challenged but changed through this life-impacting book. Its rich blend of autobiographical, spiritual and therapeutic writing give readers a strategy to walk out God's redemptive and restorative plan for their lives.

Bishop Michael E. Dantley

This is the only photo Lucreta has of herself as a child.
She is the one on the far right edge of the photo.

Section One:

My Journey

⊱━◆━○━◆━⊰

Introduction
Mustering Up the Courage

*Things can happen in childhood that set us on a
collision course with life.*

You and I live in a dangerous society. Things can happen in childhood that set us on a collision course with life. Before the age of fifteen I was abandoned, sexually molested, a runaway, and unjustly placed in a mental hospital. By the time I was a young adult, my *reaction* to these events caused me to be imprisoned five times. I was angry. I was frustrated. I was devastated. With all of the guilt, depression and shame I was feeling, it was difficult for me to even desire change, much less *"Have the Courage to Change!"*

Looking back at all of the things that happened to me, and *all* of the people I could blame, I realized that the person who had caused the most damage and inflicted most of my pain in my life was *me*. You're probably wondering how I can possibly believe this. You might want to sit me in a

If you don't want to change, put this book down.

psychiatrist's chair and tell me that what happened to me was not my fault. You'd be wasting your time. I already know that.

One day, I came to understand that after these horrible events occurred in my life, *I began to abuse myself.* I'm sure you've heard about all kinds of abuse: drug abuse, verbal abuse, sexual abuse, mental abuse, etc., but *self-abuse* is something I would like you to consider as you read this book. *Abuse* is defined by Webster's Dictionary as: *improper use, maltreatment, to insult, to revile, to pervert.* I'm going to define self-abuse as: *treating yourself*

19

improperly, insulting or reviling (hating) yourself; and even bringing yourself into perversion. **It is the negative response or reaction we have to adverse circumstances that manifests in self-injury.** We abuse ourselves all of the time. Unfortunately, we don't realize it, and it is the one thing in our lives we really can change.

I did not have the power to change my mother who abandoned me, the person who raped me, or those who put me into the mental institution. I could not change anyone who made decisions that affected me negatively and brought adversity into my life. *I was the only person I had the power to change!* Instead, I chose to continue the cycle of abuse I had experienced all my life by mistreating myself. At a certain point I had to get off the merry-go-round, or should I say "miserable-go-round" and stop the cycle. I had to stir up the courage to change the mindsets that up until then had only brought me a self-fulfilling prophecy of misery. I had to conclude that I would stop responding and reacting to the decisions of others and my fear of being hurt by them, and begin to live my own life and make my own choices.

Today, you can come to this conclusion in your own life. For some, your life has been a mental, emotional and even physical incarceration. You have literally delivered yourself into a prison. You've sentenced yourself to punishments you feel you deserve because someone in your life thought so little of you that they abused you. Surely, you have determined, *"I must not be worth anything. If I were, this would not have happened to me."* Many TV talk shows and counselors guide us into confronting our abusers as a pathway to courage and freedom. I want to suggest to you if you really want to face your worst abuser, look in the mirror and confront yourself. Then, read the rest of this book and it will help you through the process of change.

The purpose of this book is not only to tell you how I found the courage to change, but to help you change your own life. If you want to change, this book is for you. If you are called to help others change, this book is for you.

If you don't want to change, put this book down. If you have the courage to continue, you will be able to look into this book and reflect on your own life, while riding as a passenger on someone else's journey. However, to actually see change in your own life, eventually you'll have to switch seats and assume the driver's position. You will have to desire to look deeper than the surface and make decisions that will bring quality to your life.

Change is a lifetime commitment. We are constantly changing. It is a process. At no time in our lives are we allowed to sit back and say, *"I've arrived!"* When I went through the early stages of change I was isolated. I had to deal *with myself, by myself.* One of my reasons for writing this book is to let you know that you can do it alone if you need to. Sometimes we avoid change because we feel we must have some man or woman to look to, and that may or may not happen. You can walk through these steps and change alone, but there also may be people to help you if you need it. Can you be free? Yes, you can. Freedom is a choice.

We opened the doors to *Having The Courage To Change* in 1997. *Having The Courage To Change* is a program that provides structured transitional living to women who seek to recover from life-controlling behaviors. Our holistic approach offers discipleship, life-skills training and individualized treatment in a residential setting. Since the program opened, we've had a few hundred women come through the program. Out of that great number of women, many have changed certain aspects of their lives, but few have successfully endured to the end to see a total and radical change. Many quit, having neither the hunger nor the discipline it takes to persevere to the end for the sake of change. They have the courage to begin, but not to finish. They don't realize that it takes time to "undo" what has been done. It may have taken you twenty years to get into bondage. It's going to take more than twenty minutes to get out.

Applications

*Other people's decisions affect your life,
but your decisions affect it most.*

~ What have you experienced that started you on a cycle of
self-abuse?

~ Your anger is a manifestation of hurt and pain. You must have
the courage to face and feel hurt in order to be free. Feeling the
pain will give you the freedom to face your past and the future
and will propel you into understanding why you have reacted the
way you have. Are you willing to feel the pain?

~ What events have caused you to feel pain or have caused you to
suppress pain and act out in other ways?

Chapter One

Here I was, in prison for the fifth time.

I never had a real job because I was a professional thief. The last time I was in prison for theft, I served my time with ease. I did not care about what was happening to me or why. I was content in prison. This time I was in for selling drugs. I was thirty-two years old and my son was already nine. I was used to serving prison sentences and I'd planned on doing what I had always done: work the system, establish myself in the population, seek out a homosexual relationship, and prepare to just serve out my time.

This time was different. I found myself unable to do any of the usual things. It was the most difficult time I'd ever had in prison. I was facing a three-to-fifteen-year incarceration. I was agitated. I was uncomfortable. I didn't want to be locked up.

When I had served time before I was almost happy to do it. It was a way of life. I would serve my sentence and leave, not owing anyone anything. When my sentence was finished, I would go back out on the street and do what I loved: stealing. But this wasn't the same. I had been sentenced to concurrent terms by three hard judges in three different Ohio counties. Because I was a repeat offender, the system intended for me to serve out every second of my term.

"You will never have definition and meaning until you come back to the source."

I was horrified at the thought of spending fifteen more years of my life in prison. I didn't even want to spend fifteen more minutes there. I was accustomed to the routine and knew how to navigate through the system. Because I had been in a mental institution before, I knew what mental illness looked like and what behaviors signified certain types of attacks. So I faked attacks to get out of lock-up and be sent to the infirmary. I had done this successfully many times before. I could do one for you now if you could see me. I used this to get over, until the doctor discovered I was lying and stated frankly to me that I would be in big trouble if I feigned an attack again. It had been years since my mental illness "misdiagnosis," but two events that happened after that actually made me think I was going crazy.

First, I was in my cot one night trying desperately to sleep, and I heard a voice. It said, *"You will never have definition and meaning until you come back to the source."* I had no idea what that meant.

Then, a week later, I was sitting outside in the recreation area, surrounded by fences and security walls. I kept staring at the barbed wire fences and suddenly, I saw a little girl with her hands grasping the fence staring at me. Again, I heard the voice say, *"You will never have definition and meaning until you come back to the source."*

I still didn't know what the voice was trying to tell me or what the vision of the little girl meant. But forty-five days later I was miraculously given super-shock probation and released from prison. I didn't know at the time that the voice I had heard and the vision I saw would set a new course for my life. I only knew that I was being set free from jail. *I didn't realize that the voice inside was God calling me out of my condition to Him and to a better quality of life.* I didn't know that I was the little girl on the fence, and my life was hanging in the balance. *Which side of the fence would I be on? Would I be locked up for the rest of my life or would I be free?*

I had been incarcerated five times and was being released from a long-term prison sentence. I was relieved and stunned. I was free from prison. I vowed never to return, even though all of the trappings that got me into prison were still on the outside, and on the inside. I was fooling myself because the real and strongest incarceration was in my own mind.

I had no power to resist the temptations that would be presented. I had not even delved into why I had been so shackled in my mind that I became a drug dealer, a thief and lesbian. *Until I freed myself internally I would continue to live out the lifestyle and produce the fruit of an incarcerated, imprisoned mind.*

I was still a little girl behind bars.

Application

~ Are you ready to make a lifetime commitment to change?

Chapter Two

The little girl was born in 1960 and abandoned by
her birth mother.

My birthmother told her co-worker that her pregnancy was unwanted and that she was planning to give me up for adoption. Her co-worker asked if she could have me, and my mother consented. It wasn't a legal adoption, nor did the arrangement go through the foster care system. Even so, I was a foster child.

The fact that I was a foster child was not hidden from me. My foster mother constantly made mention of my birth mother to me. It wasn't until I saw a picture of my birth mother with her other children (my brothers and sisters), that I became bitter. I began to ask my foster mother

I started my cycle of self-abuse with this thought, "I have to take care of myself. I can't trust anyone to do anything for me.

why I had been given up. She didn't really have an answer for me, she just told me to be happy that I was with her. I immediately changed from a contented child to a bitter and rebellious one. Once I understood that my birth mother didn't want me, I began to resent my foster mother. In fact, I hated her, and rebelled against her authority. My hatred grew when she would respond to my revolts by beating me hard and often.

My foster mother had a boyfriend. He seemed nice at first, but things began to change. On Saturdays, I would wind up alone in the house with him while my foster mother was working. My foster brothers and sisters would be out of the house doing their own thing. The sexual abuse began when I was six and a half years old. When I was eight, he penetrated me for the first time.

My response was to run away from home. I would lie to my friends' parents, saying that I had permission to spend the night at their homes. I tried everything I knew to stay away from him. I would be gone for days! When I finally did go home, my foster mother would beat me again and again. This cycle continued for years.

Once, I did muster up the courage to tell my foster mother why I was running away. Her boyfriend had already warned me that if I ever told her what was happening, she would never believe me. She would always and only believe him. To prove that she would take his side instead of mine, he planted two dollars in my room and told my foster mother that I had stolen his money. She believed him without hesitation. It didn't matter that their relationship was stormy. One day he said to me secretly, *"I told you, whatever I say goes!"* I was totally incapacitated. The torture continued over the years; so did the running away.

When they reported that I was a runaway, the judicial system assumed that I must have had a mental problem. Certainly, no child would run from such a good home environment! I was sent to a mental hospital for evaluation and treatment that was to last for about six months. I was there for two years.

At the former Longview Mental Hospital, the patients didn't get a lot of therapy, just a lot of medication. There were so many sick children there. Although I had run away because I was being abused and molested, at Longview, I was diagnosed mentally ill. The doctors did not try to dig deeper into why I was running. No one asked what was happening at home. No one discussed my feelings of fear, pain or abandonment.

I was given shock treatments and was on liquid Thorazine for two years. I was a walking zombie who wasn't getting help for her problems. I weighed eighty pounds when I went into Longview; after fourteen months there I weighed 198 lbs!

I kept telling the doctors that I was only supposed to be in for short-term treatment. My foster mother even tried to get me out, but I was caught in the system. At age fourteen, I was finally released into a world I no longer knew, with people who no longer knew me. I was a terribly overweight teenager with no confidence, no sense of who I was, no friends and no hope. The only positive thing was that my foster mother's boyfriend was now gone.

Many things happened after the day I returned home from the mental hospital. I was forever changed. I no longer trusted authority. Everyone in authority who was supposed to protect me, from my birth and foster mothers to the judges and doctors, had left me to fight and fend for myself. I started my cycle of self-abuse with this thought, *"I have to take care of myself. I can't trust anyone to do anything for me."*

Applications

~ List the negative events that have set the abusive course of your life and are motivating your desire to change.

~ How did you respond or react to these events? Did they become a self-fulfilling prophecy (e.g. I was abandoned as a child, then I abandoned my child)?

~ What thoughts are locked up in your mind because of your experiences?

~ Did you make any vows? If so, what are they?

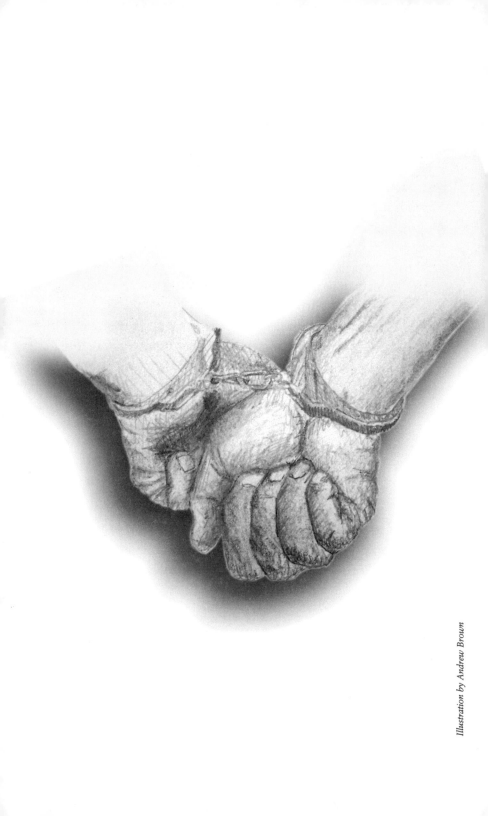

Chapter Three

*When my foster mother finally brought me back home from the
institution, her boyfriend was gone.*

It would seem that his absence would have relaxed me. I would
surely be more trusting, since the immediate threat of danger was
gone. Though I was physically free from his abuse, I was still
mentally captive in a prison of memories. I had long before lost
trust in everyone and everything.

I stayed with my foster mother because I really had nowhere else
to go. In some strange way deep down inside, I felt that I needed her.
In fact I was sure of it, despite what I had suffered, because I wasn't
ready to face the world alone. So I couldn't leave her, at least not
physically. Instead I left her inwardly, becoming more and more
rebellious. I erected my own walls, locked my own gates and shut
myself in. The epitaph on my deadened psyche read:

"No one can hurt me. I can trust no one but myself to take
care of me. I am against
everyone and everyone is
against me."

The year was 1974
and I was angry. We were
poor. My foster mother
was making only

**No one can hurt me. I can trust
no one but myself to take care of
me. I am against everyone and
everyone is against me.**

minimum wage. I was conscious of lack and need for the first time.
To fuel my anger, on Sundays at church I would watch my foster
mother give away "our money" in offering collection plates. It
seemed to me like she was giving more to the church than she was to

me. I became preoccupied with getting money by any means. Against my foster mother's wishes and decrees, I would hustle pop bottles throughout the neighborhood and turn them in for a nickel at the grocery store. Since I was breaking her rules, I had to sneak around and lie about my whereabouts.

One night, my foster mother went out and ordered me to stay in the house. I wanted money so badly that I ignored her command and ventured down the street to ask the neighbors for pop bottles. At one lady's home, I dropped a bottle. It shattered into pieces on the floor. When I knelt to clean up the glass I cut my knee very deeply. I still have the scar today. At the time I was so bent on completing my rounds and getting that money that I didn't realize how badly I was cut, or that I was bleeding, until the store clerk saw the blood and responded frantically.

I quickly limped home, all the while trying to conjure up an excuse for the terrible cut. I decided to tell my foster mother that I had accidentally cut myself on a pop bottle that had broken under *our own* kitchen sink. She instantly knew I was lying and reminded me that she never kept pop bottles under the sink in her house. She had to rush me to the emergency room where I received twenty-six stitches in my knee. As soon as we returned home, even though I was hurt and had stitches, she beat me once again with an extension cord. I decided then and there that if I ever got another beating, it would be for something big.

About thirty days later, I was uptown in the shopping district selling candy for a school fundraiser. I was just wandering around looking inside the shops. The weather was growing colder, so I walked into a department store to warm up and spotted a pair of white earmuffs. I wanted those earmuffs badly. They were so white and clean and soft. I began to devise a plan to steal them. I walked around the store for a half hour planning the theft and my escape. I decided to grab the earmuffs quickly and put them in my candy box. Surely no one would spot me. They wouldn't care about one pair of earmuffs anyway. I stealthily carried out my plan and was cautiously walking toward the exit when a security guard stopped me. "Miss...I need you to come to the office with me," he said. He led me to a back room. I was stunned. I couldn't believe that I was caught. I had planned the crime so perfectly. The thought of facing the police scared me to death. It was superseded only by the fear of facing my foster mother.

The security guard questioned me. Then he lectured me about the dangers of shoplifting, stating that it was a serious crime. Because I was so young and had never shoplifted before, I was allowed to leave in my foster mother's custody without any charges being filed against me. She was so shocked that I had gone that far that she didn't even beat me. She only reprimanded me verbally and placed me on punishment for stealing. Though she never wanted to talk about it, I believe that she felt guilty about all the time I had spent in the mental hospital. Surely I had to be crazy! Now I was a crazy thief.

I was never allowed back in the store. I was warned that if I were caught there, I would immediately be taken to prison. I deceived

The fact that I was evading, scheming and fighting against authority proved beyond a shadow of a doubt that I was definitely under authority.

myself into thinking that my ingenuity had gotten me out of that bad situation. I had escaped prison, so I was fearless. I thought I was totally in control and that "the powers that be" couldn't touch me. I vowed to become so excellent at stealing and lying that I would never be caught again. I could not see at the time, that *I was not running a single thing.*

My rebellion against the concept of authority only proved that authority existed, and I needed it. It's a bit like the atheist who fights God, stating that they don't believe in Him. The fact that they are fighting so hard against God demonstrates a belief in God. If there were no God, there would be no need to fight against Him.

This period in my life was a battle of wills raging inside of me. I had lost control because I was so full of anger, bitterness and resentment. I resisted the control of others so strongly that I didn't realize that my strong resistance authenticated and solidified their control over me. All I could focus on was what "*they*" had done to me. If I had just been able to let "*them*" go, I would have gained control of myself and unlocked my own prison doors.

Applications

~ Though you may be physically free, in what area(s) are you still mentally in prison?

~ What epitaph (statement placed over a person's grave) did you write and begin to live out in your own life?

~ Who are you blaming? Who have you held responsible for the bad things that happened to you?

~ What (or who) are you attempting to control that is really controlling you?

Chapter Four

Six months after my release from the mental hospital,
the weight I had gained began to fall off.

The boys in my neighborhood began to notice me and I liked it. So I used my body to control my male companions. Some of the boys I made out with wanted to have real relationships with me, but I absolutely refused. If I could control nothing else, I could at least control who I was going to be with and when. I refused to commit. I was nobody's girlfriend.

My rebellion against authority continued. I had not yet mastered the craft of thievery so I was caught again and again. For the next five years I was in and out of jail and juvenile centers for theft and robbery. In an odd sort of way this benefited me. Had I not been locked up, I never would have received my secondary education. At the Riverview School for Girls my days were organized and structured. I was a good student who excelled in classes. I did not, however, learn anything about how to live life in a productive way.

Sadly, the angry me was not the real me. It was just a facade strategically placed like the first line of soldiers in a battle.

Anger was still controlling me. It was with me like an old friend. I was constantly brawling. I was put in isolation more times than I wish to count for fighting. Now I know that anger is just a mask for hurt and disappointment. I was using anger to defend my heart from the pain, rejection and abandonment that it had endured. I had built a fortress to keep people away from the wounded little girl inside.

I was like a chameleon during my time at Riverview. This is the behavior of many rejected and abandoned children. When you are a child, your circle of influence is *yourself*. If something *good* happens, *you* did it! If something *bad* happens, *you* did it and it's *your* fault! You do not have the ability to reason as an adult. You cannot see motives nor do you understand reasons why. If everything good is you and everything bad is you, then you adjust your behavior so that everyone around you will only perceive your actions as good. Then, you will always be liked and no one will reject, abuse or leave you again. If behaving badly will gain acceptance, you do that. If being perfect and excelling in school will win over your teachers, you do that. I was beginning to master "doing this and that."

There was a rank-and-file system among my peers at Riverview. I fit into that system by doing exactly what I needed to do and being who I needed to be. In a setting of incarceration (and in an incarcerated mind, I might add), you will see the imagination manipulate its world to simulate the norm. Since there were no boys and no families at Riverview, only girls, we simulated opposite sex relationships. This led me into a homosexual relationship with a senior in the school from whom I received the acceptance, protection and care that I had failed to get from my foster mother. Though I participated in this relationship, I never really saw myself as a homosexual at the time. I was just a chameleon. I was doing whatever I needed to do to get what I wanted. Eventually, this pattern became so ingrained in me that I actually began to believe I was a homosexual from birth and could not help or change my behavior.

My case manager at Riverview called me in one day. He said I had committed so many crimes and the State had spent so much money on me that I was *"a menace to society."* A menace to society! It was a blow to my psyche. I allowed that statement to control me for years. They say that if you tell a child they are no good, or they will end up "just like their daddy," the statement becomes a self-fulfilling prophecy. Well, "a menace to society" stuck to me like glue.

My case manager went on to say that he would be recommending that I be put out of the State of Ohio! "The State," he said, "shouldn't have to pay another dime for you to go to school and receive help when you aren't going to do anything with it." He proclaimed that I would *never* be anything. I retaliated with, *"You don't know what you're talking about and you don't know me!"* I ranted and raved, but at age sixteen, I was banished from the State of Ohio. I did not return until I was twenty-eight.

My foster mother and I had to move to Kentucky. Her life was being turned upside-down, so she was angry and upset. I was angry, too, because I had no control over my situation. At least some of her family was from Kentucky, so she had connections. I, on the other hand, knew no one. I became more resentful and rebellious and I was still stealing.

I was caught again and placed in Juvenile Hall in Lexington for eight months. When I returned home, I was shocked to find that my foster mother was dating her ex-husband. I was unaware that she had a man other than her abusive boyfriend. She had never mentioned that she was married before, but I saw that this relationship was very different. She showed her ex-husband no respect. She was fully in control. I was relieved because there would be no abuse, but my attention had turned to my own "love life."

At seventeen, I found a man who had everything I didn't: a car, possessions, and money and he was willing to share them with me. I grew to love and respect him for making his own way without having to depend on anyone else. He worked, he was responsible, and he was disciplined. I began to emulate his discipline by controlling the only thing I felt I could, my own body. I became obsessed with weight, because staying small is what I believed had attracted him to me. I shrank from a size twelve to a size two.

Everything seemed to be going well. I was in love, I was small and then I became pregnant and would soon have a child by the man I loved. In my sixth month of pregnancy, I was in the bathtub and my water broke. I was alone at the time because my foster mother was out walking the dog. The baby came out stillborn. I felt that I was to blame because I was so concerned with keeping my weight down that I never ate enough to nourish the baby. It was such a loss for me. The anger and control that I had worked so hard to get was causing me to implode; it was turning my body against me. Years later, I found out that the reason for the stillbirth (and the loss of two other babies) was the sexual abuse I had endured as a child. The damage to my body and emotions had already been done.

The relationship fell apart after the death of our child. At first, my lover began to abuse me physically. Then I caught him in bed with another woman. I was so disappointed. He was the one person I believed was different, and he turned out to be just like everyone else. I left him. Then he wanted me back so badly that he began to stalk me. I told my foster mother what was going on and for the first time she protected me! She told me what to do to curtail the stalking: *simply ignore him*. It sounds so simple and uncomplicated, but it worked. All I did was pretend I didn't see him. Even though we would encounter one another at the store or on the street corner, I simply ignored him. He did silly things to get my attention and when he saw it wouldn't work, he got angry and called me names. I ignored the name-calling too, and after a few months the relationship just faded away. I never had any more trouble with him. Though the issue of lovers was temporarily on hold, my illegal pursuits continued.

From age eighteen to nineteen I was in a theft ring and eventually became its leader. Our motto was: *"there is no honor among thieves."* This was true; we would even steal from one another. I would tell my thieving apprentices, *"Don't trust me if I'm teaching you to steal."* We would steal from each other, and say, *"It's not personal."*

I planned thefts meticulously. I would mentally put myself in the position of the detectives: imagining what they would do to solve the crime. Then I would lay the plan out on a table and sketch how the operation should take place. I was creating my own world, and in my world, I was winning.

That was until I was caught. But this time I wasn't underage. I determined that I *was not* going to prison for 2-1/2 years! I told the authorities I was seventeen. They couldn't lock up a minor. They would just put me on probation or another tolerable punishment. I was instructed to bring in my birth certificate so that my age could be verified. No problem! I would just forge the date on the document and I would be free.

I obtained the document and used "Wite-Out" to change my birth date. I brought it to the Clerk of Courts for verification. Everything was going smoothly and I just knew I would be out of there in no time. The next thing I knew, the Sheriff was handcuffing me! He read me my rights and told me I was being arrested for criminal possession of a forged document. In a split second, I went from being in charge, on top and in control, to facing five years in prison. I immediately realized that though I had changed my birth date on the birth certificate, I had neglected to change the date that accompanied the doctor's signature. Oh well, I thought, I'll serve the time, get out and go back to what I was doing. Next time, I'll be smarter and I won't get caught. Then I'll be in control again.

Applications

~ How have you behaved like a chameleon to fit other people's expectations?

~ Have you blamed yourself as a child for something in your life that as an adult you realize was not your fault?

~ Was there a statement made to or about you that caused you to choose the wrong path in your fork in the road?

~ What event(s) planted your seed of distrust, doubt and insecurity?

~ How have these things affected your relationships with the opposite sex?

~ Have you engaged in activities thinking you're in control and on top of the world, only to find you were deceiving yourself? Explain.

Chapter Five

Until age thirty-two, the little girl behind the bars
controlled my every move.

I didn't realize it then, but all of the decisions I had made up to that point had been chain reactions to, or rebellions against what that little girl had experienced. My emotional responses to the abuse and molestation led to distrust and running away, which led to trying to gain control, which was immediately followed by scamming and illegal activity.

Once I was told that I was a menace to society, though everything in my heart wanted to prove the statement wrong, my emotional reactions made it happen.

I was aging chronologically, but that little girl was still running the show. A grown woman with a little girl's heart and mind! There is an old Bible verse that says (my paraphrase), *"When I was a child, I thought like a child, I spoke like a child, I reasoned like a child. But when I became a (woman), I put away childish things."* (I Cor. 13:11) I was handling mature, grown-up situations with the feelings and reasoning of a little child. My interpretations were childish. I needed the adult me to step in. I had to heal that little girl and introduce her to the grown-up me: the one that would take us through the rest of our life. I let her know that what had happened to her was not her fault, that there was nothing wrong with her and

I don't know if I had ever had an original thought — one that just came from me.

that she did not do anything to cause the abuses that she experienced. I thanked her for the good job she did in helping me to survive, but now I had to live, and she wasn't equipped to take us to that level. Now I wanted to feel the pain and not run, but grow from it. I wanted to be able to rise above my hurt and not have to medicate it.

Still, the disappointment I experienced was just a foretaste of what was to come. My path seemed set on total self-destruction. My problems stemmed from a bad self-image and abandonment, and they were overwhelming. I did not realize that poor self-worth and abandonment were like two lenses on a pair of glasses; if you have them on, you see everything from their magnified viewpoint. When you look at a person, you see them despising you. You see them leaving you for no reason, even if that's not their true intent. That might not be the case for you. You could be dealing with totally different issues. *What are the lenses in your glasses? What do they tell you? How are you going to change?*

In 1979, I was in prison serving a three to five year sentence for theft with a forged instrument. It was mixed with maximum and minimum-security inmates. My concept of prison from TV, movies and things I had heard, was one of rape, beatings and gangs, so when I went there I was focused on not projecting fear. Those glasses can really project images that are not there! In truth, I had nothing to worry about because I fit right in with the other inmates. The population was primarily made up of repeat offenders and we spent most of our time telling "war stories." I didn't have any "beat downs," just petty arguments.

The Correctional Institute I was in was not "*correcting*" anything in me. I was just there to be held. I didn't have any visitors, not even my foster mother. She didn't believe in visiting folks in jail, so my "family" was in prison with me. We created a mother, father, sisters, brothers and cousins to make a surrogate life like the one we had on the outside.

I actually felt comfortable in prison because I was creating my own little ideal world and it was safe - or at least familiar. I felt I needed to be in prison because at least I had a *"dependable family"* there. Deep down, I guess I knew it wasn't real, but the mind is so strong that even now in retrospect I have to *guess*.

When I recounted this story to those who were assisting me to write this book, my mind had so tricked me that prison life conjured up more pleasant memories than "freedom" did. I felt more locked up outside of prison than in prison. To the great surprise of my literary cohorts, adjustment seemed easier to me when I was in prison. Living outside scared me to death and was much harder to me. These were signs that I was still mentally incarcerated in some ways, even though I was free on the outside. My mind was locked in a state of false reality.

I served only eighteen months of the sentence because the prison was overcrowded. They had to let some of us out. I was released for "good behavior."

I wasn't sent to any type of halfway house to re-acclimate myself with the outside. I had no marketable skills; I stole for a living. My foster mother had moved back to Ohio, so I lived with my aunt in Kentucky and then with a friend. I had no support system, so I just went back to the things I knew. I was caught again. I had violated parole so I was sent back to prison for two years to complete my initial sentence. I didn't care, because by then I was totally frustrated with life on the outside.

You don't have to be physically incarcerated to accept what is unreal as more real than reality. Children who are abandoned by their parents, victims of adultery and divorce, people with sicknesses, etc. often view themselves through eyes of unworthiness. They see themselves as less valuable than they are, and lock themselves inside the gate of their own mental perceptions. Friends and family, counselors and pastors make attempts to unlock their cells with the truth, but they are unable to hear it, unable to see themselves in any other way than through their victimization.

Because of my childhood experiences (abuse, molestation and the mental ward), I looked at life through lenses of fear and distrust.

My reactions to everything were driven by fear. It was the warden of my prison. I was afraid to be abused, so I ran. I was afraid to trust, so I controlled. I was too afraid to face reality and change, so I was happy being a thief and going back to prison!

I finished the sentence, was released and moved back in with my aunt. This time, I willed to make a new start. I focused on being successful and I even got a job working with handicapped children. But the past still claimed a part of me: I continued to steal. I wasn't as sure of my ability to live in the "free" world as I was about my skills in the incarcerated world. I wanted to make sure that I would survive. A part of me just didn't want to let it go. This was my identity! I could devise a plan to steal and not get caught because I was a master thief (at least in my own mind).

One night I went to a nightclub with a friend and her brother. I didn't think he would be interested in me because I knew he went for glamorous college girls with long hair. I was the total opposite! I was shocked and elated when this man pursued and wooed me. He treated me so tenderly and lovingly - like no one ever had before. He also knew I was a thief, but he never challenged me to stop. We started a relationship. Now my life was really coming together!

We got our own apartment and car, and we were going to make it. I was going through the motions of a normal person, but life seemed unreal. Fear gripped me. It told me I could never be happy or whole. Fear began to drive and control me, and I didn't have the tools to free myself from its clutches. Fear drove me to cheat on the man with whom I was attempting to build a normal life.

We were together for eight months when I succumbed to temptation and had an affair with another man. I met him at the same nightclub where I had met my boyfriend. He was a very popular, older man. I wanted the affair because my boyfriend would not tell me that he loved me. He showed by his actions that he cared, but I wanted desperately to hear those words. I took this older man to our apartment one night and my boyfriend came home and caught us in bed together. A fight broke out. I felt unusually strong because they were fighting over me! No one had ever cared enough to fight for me before. I didn't know how to do the *right* thing in this situation, so I did what I knew...I played these two good-looking men against each other. I was living in fear and fantasy at the same time. Still, a small voice inside me was telling me that this was all unreal.

I got pregnant again; it was unbelievable! My chances of conceiving a child were next to none, and I was surprised that I had another chance to bring a life into the world. I had to face the drama I had caused. When I told my boyfriend I was pregnant, he said he couldn't be sure the child was his. Could I blame him? I knew this child was his and I did everything I could to keep our relationship together.

He decided to stay with me and I was so glad. The doctor told me that I had to have an operation for my incompetent cervix and uterus. My past was coming back to haunt me again. The abuse I'd suffered was ruining my chances of having a baby. I went ahead with the procedure and it was successful. My boyfriend was with me the whole time and it helped to build our relationship. We were together and I was happy. We had a son.

For the first time life seemed worth living to me. My foster mother came to stay with me for two weeks after my son was born. My boyfriend was attentive and happy too. Everything was just perfect until the cycle of self-abuse returned. I slid back into destructive behavior.

Have you ever experienced the ebb-and-flow of the cycle of self-abuse? You ignore the root of your problem and temporarily medicate or anesthetize it. Time passes and you think everything's alright — you're handling it. Then one day a situation comes that taps into that wounded place just to let you know — *"Baby, I'm still here, you haven't really dealt with me, so I'm going to deal with you."* Until you stop this cycle, you are not free, nor have you changed; you are still locked up in your prison!

My son was ten months old when I got involved in drugs. I never really saw it as wrong. I was in control of my life. As long as I was directing myself, nothing I did seemed wrong or out of bounds. For two years I did drugs and kept on stealing. When my son was three, I was sent to prison once again for theft by deception: stealing and signing checks. Another turn of the cycle!

Even though I had a toddler, a boyfriend, and seemingly a new life, here I was doing my third time in prison! I was devastated because I was losing control. It wasn't about seeing old friends this time. I wanted out.

I didn't have any status at this prison because I didn't know most of the other inmates. You gain control in prison by getting close to the staff, using your body for sex, getting into cliques, and manipulating and lying. Since I had no status that would give me power, I gained control by refusing to eat. In six months I went from being a size twelve, due to my

Now, I wondered if I had sabotaged myself in order to be caught so that I could return to the familiar and comfortable state of incarceration.

pregnancy, down to a size two. I had anorexia, a new level of self-abuse. It was the only way for me to be in charge of something. My boyfriend came to visit me sometimes and I even joined a parenting group so that my son could stay overnight with me on occasion.

After one year, I was let out of prison. My boyfriend gave my son back to me, but he left. He didn't want anything else to do with me.

After all of those stays in prison I had not been rehabilitated nor had I been corrected. I was out and I still had no support system, and no way to stay out of prison and off of drugs. Surprisingly enough, I still felt I had control of myself even though I had spent more time in prison than out. I had deceived myself into thinking I was an invincible thief that would never get caught. That *obviously* was not the case.

I got caught changing price tags and was sent to prison to serve *every day of a ten-year sentence*. I was living up to those prophecies about me. I was good for nothing but the prison system.

I went to prison feeling settled because it felt like home. The other inmates and I just reacted to our situation. We lied to ourselves by saying, "We'll just make our own reality." We were functioning addicts and okay with it. Can you imagine being addicted to prison? "feenin" for incarceration like a druggie? Our bodies were incarcerated, but more than that, our minds were locked up! We sentenced ourselves to life and didn't see anything wrong with it. It might be easy for you to be smug about my story until you begin to think of the ways that you have sentenced yourself to a life of mediocrity, depression, and failure.

After serving four years of my ten-year sentence they decided to release me back into society. I was afraid to leave prison this time. There, I had rules to live by and boundaries to live within. Those things weren't available to me on the outside. Something else happened right before I was released that frightened me to my core.

My cellmate, Ms. Francis, died of a heart attack right in our cell. I heard her gasping and saw her writhing but I couldn't do anything to save her. The guards didn't make it to her in time. The state authorities had to close out her sentence because she died while doing time. She remained in a body bag for eight hours…in our cell…with me still there. I was there the entire time with a dead, bound up body in the cell with me. Her family didn't even come to claim her body.

I thought to myself…

"We all die in our prisons, and this woman has died not ever being free!"

I was so shaken that I went to speak with the chaplain. I was afraid to leave because *I began to realize that my mind was in prison*. He told me something I will never forget…

"Fear will keep you cautioned. Not being fearful, aware of the damage that can be done if you get off track, is your enemy. Being afraid will keep you inside of boundaries."

Armed with the knowledge that a certain kind of fear could help me, I was ready to start over again. I didn't know the desperate, deep, dark place into which I was headed.

What happened next broke me. I got out of prison ready to restore and repair relationships, but time had run out. My foster mother died suddenly in May of 1989. I had lost my chance to rebuild a relationship with her. I realized too late that I actually *did* love my foster mother. I couldn't even get relief or mourn at the funeral because my life had been so destructive. When I was introduced to the pastor as "the bad sister," deeply buried feelings of abandonment and uselessness overwhelmed me. Not only was I called "bad" because of the choices I made, but also because I had uprooted our family when my foster mother and I went to Kentucky to live after I got put out of the State of Ohio. I hadn't realized what that did to her other children.

Now my only stabilizing force was my son. It was just about time for him to go back to school when his father told me that I couldn't keep him any longer and there was no way I would ever have him again. I was so desperate that I envisioned kidnapping my son and running away. I couldn't go through with it. I loved him too much to put him through another ordeal.

I went to court. I really didn't know why I was there. Surely the judge would realize that a child was better off with his mother. I expected to get full custody of my son, but instead, we were ripped apart. His father denounced me as unfit and unstable. My rap sheet told a story that could not be denied. I'd lost everything in one year: my boyfriend, my mother, my son, my home, and my car.

I attempted to take care of a young cousin of mine who had no home and no one to take care of her. She would be my substitute child. It was a big mistake, because I had nothing to give the little girl and I was not prepared for the responsibility. I had to surrender her to my family.

It was 1990 and this had been my longest stretch out of prison. I was selling crack and I was with an IV drug user with whom I'd had a lesbian relationship in prison. I was completely out and unashamed. Before, I hadn't "felt" like a lesbian because I was doing what I needed to do to get acceptance and protection, now I physically and emotionally desired that kind of relationship with another woman. It was "my orientation." I was broken and defeated and didn't know how to get out. My rationale for continuing in my behavior was...

"I tried to do it the right way, but it didn't work!"

Applications

~ Stealing was a reaction to being out, even though I didn't want to go back to jail. What are some of your reactions? What triggers them?

~ You are a genuine person with creative ideas, responses and original thoughts. What can trigger you now to be that unique person?

~ When you have been "thrown away" you begin to devalue yourself and others. Accepting yourself can bring back worth and value. Write 5 things you value about yourself.

~ What are the lenses through which you see events in your world? What aspects of being bound in the familiar make you more comfortable than being free? What scares you about freedom?

Chapter Six

Trying, but not successful

I was in prison for the fifth time – this time for selling drugs. The other four times I was incarcerated in the same facility, but this time the location was different. I didn't see the same people or guards. I wasn't familiar with my surroundings and I felt totally out of place. I was desperate, lonely and depressed. I decided that I would fake my way out.

My plan was to fake a seizure so I would be put on medication. That way, I could sleep through the entire three-to-fifteen years. I was thirty-one and I had lost everything. The prosecutor and my probation officer said I wasn't getting out of prison until I had served my full sentence. The thought of serving that length of time was unbearable to me. The only way I saw myself completing this sentence was to be drugged-up.

I faked a seizure one day and it worked! Everyone believed me and I got a lot of special attention. I didn't have to be with the other inmates; I could just rest in the infirmary. I planned on doing my entire sentence in this unreal, made-up state. I would be the consummate actress!

"You will never have definition and meaning in your life until you come back to the source."

The second time I faked a seizure I almost killed myself. We were out in the yard and I took a bunch of Valium pills given to me by the infirmary. I acted out what the medics were saying and simulated the symptoms. I heard them say, "Her pulse is racing." So I made myself breathe harder. "Her pupils will dilate." I rolled my eyes in my head. I don't know why they couldn't tell I was faking, because I made sure I fell out in the grass and not on the concrete, and I made myself foam at the mouth.

When the Valium finally kicked in I was in trouble. I actually did stop breathing. I was on life support for five days. When I woke up, the doctors said I was dead for about one minute.

About a month later, the guards told me I was ready to go back to the yard. I faked another seizure because I didn't want to go. I wanted out! They took me to the Ohio State University Hospital and I was found out. A therapist told me that my seizures were psychosomatic. She said I never had one seizure; it was all in my head. They let me stay in the hospital for ten days. I was told if I had another seizure they would just let me act out and do nothing. *They weren't wasting any more time or money on me.*

From October to January, I settled in for a long sentence. I went into survival mode. I would not allow myself to be depressed. I would conquer and control my fears and my feelings. No one would see me sweat!

I found some friends I had grown up with in Hamilton and got into a few superficial relationships. The guards were really nasty in that prison. They would just walk in on you without knocking. So I stayed to myself and remained quiet. We were in a dormitory-type setting and I was taking classes for college credit.

I didn't have any contact with my son. His father vowed that I would never see him again. No one on the outside came to see me nor did they contact me in any way.

In the tenth month of my sentence I was lying down in my dorm room. Three of my roommates were in there, too. All of a sudden, I heard the voice: *"You will never have definition and meaning in your life until you come back to the source."*

I thought, *"I am finally losing my mind! Now I'm hearing voices!"* It sounded like my own voice, but it was coming from outside of me.

The next day I was out in the yard. I saw the barbed wire fence encasing the facility. All of a sudden I saw a little girl behind the barbed wire fence looking at me. A voice said again, *"You will never have definition and meaning in your life until you come back to the source."* This time I answered back, *"If you will teach me, I am willing to learn."*

A few days later I received a letter from my lawyer. I hadn't heard from him all the time I had been in prison, and I really didn't expect to. What his letter stated was unbelievable. He said that he wanted to put me up for judicial shock probation. I couldn't believe it! When I went to prison he said there was no way I was getting out! I had resigned myself to the fact that I was going to do my whole sentence with no possibility of parole, but now a door seemed to be opening. As I continued to read the letter, my hope turned to disappointment. My lawyer wrote that he wanted to help me, but I had to do something to set everything in motion. I had to write a letter to the judge about my life and why I wanted the chance to get out of prison.

You might think that I immediately got pen and paper and began writing, but it didn't work that way. After years of disappointment and not trusting authority, I thought writing to the judge was a complete waste of time. I didn't want to recall all of the things that had happened to me. I certainly didn't want to submit myself to the judge who had put me away. My lawyer contacted me in prison twice to see if I had written the letter. I'm sure he was amazed that I was procrastinating. He explained that the reason he was even contacting me was because he wanted to be able to tell himself that he had done everything he could to help me. He said he wanted to file the motion for me as soon as possible. I guess it was his compassion that prompted me to move.

Two days later I got up and started writing. I wrote that I couldn't promise that I would never commit crime again because all I knew was that promises were made to be broken. I wrote about what I had been through. To the best of my ability, I wrote about the person I had become. I told the judge that I needed someone to teach me what to do, and if I had that someone, I would learn. I wrote that I was ready to deal with my problems and face them head on.

I wrote that letter in April and my lawyer filed the motion in May. My case was on the judge's desk waiting for him to review it. I learned later that the judge had seen my file and had pushed it away three or four times. He was familiar with what I had done and had no intention of reviewing my case, let alone releasing me. He kept moving my file further and further away from the "important" stack on his desk, but somehow my file kept coming before him.

Finally, he decided to review my case because he was tired of seeing my file on his desk. After reading my letter, the judge said that it was the most honest and real letter he had seen from someone coming to him for early probation. He decided to give me a chance. I went before the judge on June 8th and was released on August 9th. The judge said that he believed I had what it took to make it, but that the decision to remain free was completely my own.

I was free, but the battle wasn't over because I had sentences from three different judges in three different Ohio counties! The judge who gave me shock probation couldn't negate the other two judges' decisions about my life. So, even though I was free, I still had to go before those other two judges. I was arrested after only one week of being out of jail because the other two judges had not concurred with the first judge's shock probation decision. I was sent back to Marysville and it seemed like I had gotten nowhere. I was back where I'd started. I was learning firsthand how difficult it is when you want to change.

I could have given up. I could have said that I had wasted my time writing to the judge and believing that a door had opened for me. I could have said that the voice I heard was just me psyching myself out. But I didn't. This time I wasn't giving up. I gained strength and confidence when that judge said he thought I had what it took to make it. No one had ever believed in me before. I determined I was going to fight and do whatever I could to convince the other judges that I was worthy of the shock probation. After thirty days all three of the judges concurred with the shock probation decision.

On August 9th I was released and sent to a group home. Almost sixteen years earlier I had been told that I was a menace to society.

I let all the other residents know that I wasn't there to play - I was there to change. If I saw them jeopardize my good standing, I would tell on them

Now I was allowed to have another chance because someone told me that I had what it took to make it - and I believed him!

immediately. I was serious about changing my life. Some of them tried a few times just to see what I would do, and I kept my promise. I told the supervisors immediately of any inappropriate behavior that could possibly affect me.

After eighteen months, I went into counseling to finally learn how to deal with that little girl behind the bars.

As you read this you may become excited about the fact that all I had to do was write a letter to a judge and he let me out of prison. Divine providence caused it to be so for me, but it may not happen that way for you. You may view my life like an *'overnight success.'* It took seventeen years in and out of prison for me to get to a place where I could confront myself and tell the world that I was ready to change my life. Once I was ready, the opportunity arose. You may think you're ready, but maybe you're not yet. You may have faked your way through so far, telling people what they want to hear, but that is not true courage. The second part of this book will test your courage and equip you to begin to make the changes necessary to be free.

Application

~ Write a letter to yourself, telling the truth about yourself. Why should you be given a chance to change? What about this time is different from before?

Chapter Seven

The process of change begins

I got out of prison on August 9th but I had nowhere to go. My Parole Officer knew that I desperately wanted to make it this time. I sincerely wanted help. He told me about a halfway house. Unfortunately, there were no beds available. I was shocked to hear that the halfway house would only take you in if you came directly from prison. Since I had already been released, I wasn't eligible. My Parole Officer stated that the only way I could get in the halfway house would be if he locked me up again. Amazingly, I was ready! I told myself that I was being *"locked up to be broke out!"*

I was in jail for another six and a half weeks! I was alone in a cell and just spent my time talking to God. I sensed Him saying to me, *"If you'll let me, I'll take you into the dark places of your life."* I knew that meant this "process" would eventually free me even though I would have to face pain.

When you're "in process" you will find that most of the time the results you are seeking do not come instantly.

One of the very interesting things about the six and a half weeks was that it was a very peaceful time for me. Somehow, by the grace of God, I was given a cell without a roommate. This is not a usual occurrence. During this time I read the Bible for the first time. I opened the pages from Genesis 1:1 and read on. Even though I was reading God's account of creation and history that involved others, I felt a sense of foundation and continuity coming to my own life. The words in the Bible are said to be spirit and life. I found life imparted to me while reading the inspired words God gave to us through man. It was the beginning of real change for me.

I would like to add that reading, studying and most importantly *applying* what I'd read were fundamental parts of my change. It takes courage to read books that will instruct and challenge us. Many authors are purposed to assist us with life's journey. I encourage anyone in the process of healing and recovery to read books and articles, listen to self-help teachings, meditate, go to church, do whatever it takes to free your mind.

Some of the books that helped me were: *The Road Less Traveled* by Scott Peck, *The Three Battle Grounds* by Francis Frangipane, *The Release of the Spirit* and *The Spiritual Man* by Watchman Nee.

I also read a 30-day journal by Og Mandingo entitled, *The Best Salesman in the World.* During this month-long journey, you must record everything you do and how you do it. For example, *"I got up on the left side of the bed, my right foot hit the floor first, then my left...and so on."* This book taught me self-awareness and how to live in and enjoy the present moment rather than focus so much on my past or my future.

I also met a counselor at the halfway house with whom I could really relate, and from whom I could learn. I felt I needed to have her as my personal therapist, but she wasn't taking any more patients. I begged her to help me. She finally relented. During the next ninety days I mined into those deep, dark places in my life and began to see myself in a totally different light. I saw that the child in me had been making decisions, running, and subsequently *ruining* my life. *My therapist also helped me to see the good that came out of all the bad decisions.* I was abandoned but I was kept; I was abused, but not destroyed; I was hospitalized as mentally ill, but I could still think!

During this time, I learned several things. First of all, it is important for us to share our process of change with others. Meeting with this therapist allowed me to talk through the things that I had previously suppressed and acted out. It allowed me to get clarity and perspective from a person who was outside my situation. She had not been through the things that I'd experienced and was able to shine some light, or at least a different point of view on my situation and how I processed it. *Sometimes the pain of our circumstances is so great that we push it into our subconscious and it shows up through our behavior.* We never thought through the fact that we were children and the abuse was not our fault. We couldn't see through our pain that everyone has a free will. Our husband or wife could have just decided they don't want to be with us, without it being because of us. Therapists, psychologists and self-help groups get a bad rap. They are not there to tell us what to do, but to assist us in finding our own way to healing. If you are hurting and your issues are beyond the scope what your family and friends can help, find a professional and get the help you need. You don't want to spend another day bound!

Second, I found that sharing your story is freeing. In the Christian faith, we are taught that part of overcoming evil is sharing our testimony. We testify to the fact that being in relationship with God has changed us, and *"saved us"* from evil, sadness, and the despair that we were in prior to knowing Him. We share openly with others what God has done for us, and how thankful we are for His love and favor. *In this gratefulness and appreciation, we are consistently reminded that we are better off today than we were yesterday.* We have made progress and are changing. *Today* God has given us what we need to live. He will do it again *tomorrow. Because we are always in a growth process, we must put up memorial milestones to recall each progressive step.* When you were a baby, all you could do was be held, then you could hold your head up on your own, then you could crawl, then kneel, then walk, then run, etc. Good parents always celebrate each step! *"Look! Junior held up his head on his own today!"* That's the way God wants us to celebrate each aspect of our own change.

Finally, in sharing our story with others we have in-built accountability. Now everyone knows where I've been and what I've done. I told it, so you can't hold it against me. *"Did you know Lucreta used to steal?"* *"Yeah girl, she told us that yesterday. She put all the details in her book!"* No one can condemn me. They can't pull any skeletons out of my closet, because I've already opened up about everything I USED to do. I have found that my honesty has shocked many people, because they would never tell the things I've told – but that's usually why they're still not free. Free people don't mind sharing their story. They're not afraid of what you think. They're not worried they're going to go back to their former behavior, because they've *made a decision* to live differently. Now that they've disclosed what they were addicted to or involved in, AND told folks that they've committed to change, *EVERYONE is watching what they do.* If they want to hold true to their change, they will monitor their behavior at all times – when they are seen, *and in private.*

This is my only concern about the "anonymous" groups. Your identity is hidden which can take away your opportunity to testify to change in truth. You can remain ashamed and hiding if you are constantly "a recovering alcoholic," "drug addict," etc. You are never able to say "I have been freed, delivered, changed" or whatever vernacular you choose to use. I chose Christianity because I am able to say...

"My name is Lucreta Bowman and I am born again. I have been freed from drugs, lesbianism, abuse, control, theft and everything else. Now you can watch my life and see evidence that Jesus Christ, and my belief in Him is real and brings results!"

You see, true change is not about a moment and a good feeling. We do not "arrive" in our development though we may overcome in particular areas. We cannot get comfortable thinking we've crossed the finish line of the 100 meter dash when we're really running a 26 mile marathon. So many folks are putting their arms out and leaning into an invisible tape thinking they've won the victory. Not yet!

There is always something more or different that can be improved. I might not steal money anymore, but I may steal time from someone by always being late. We can acknowledge that a disrespectful and selfish person would steal money from a purse, but not time from a person! We all have to ask, *"What do I do to stay in-process and to keep growing and changing?"* Whatever it took to get you where you are, it will take double that to keep you! Change is not just for the homeless, the incarcerated and the addicted – it's for all of us!

I was released from the halfway house after ninety-three days. I moved into a women's shelter and got a part-time job at a restaurant making $4 an hour, twenty-five hours a week. When I interviewed for the job, I was completely honest about my past. Being honest and working with integrity gained me favor and qualified me for a better position. The employer wanted me to be a cashier. I knew that I wasn't ready for that, so I asked him to hire me as a hostess, and he did. While we are recovering, we have to be aware of ourselves: our strengths, weaknesses, and limitations. If you know that being around money, or alcohol, or women, etc., is a weakness for you, then while you are recovering (and sometimes indefinitely) it is best not to put yourself in that temptation. I knew I was struggling with theft and that being at that cash register would only cause that impulse to rise. I did not lie to myself and say, *"I got this. I can handle it!"* I knew that I couldn't. Even if I thought that I could, I didn't want to jeopardize my recovery or my job. I certainly did not want to take a chance at going back to prison! I believe this decision was one of my milestones and proved that I was serious about allowing myself the TIME it takes to change.

I was still in counseling with my therapist. The work was intense, focused and goal oriented. At the halfway house one of the workers approached me with a request, *"We aren't really supposed to do this, but I'm going to ask my supervisor if I can take you to church with me, if you are willing."* That church was Christ Emmanuel Christian Fellowship. When I went to the church for the first time and the altar call was given, I almost fell forward. I said to myself, *"I will learn something here."* Through the teachings I learned that homosexuality was not God's original intention. God had made woman for man. I received the grace to come out of the dark aspects of my former lifestyle.

I participated in a 12-step group with males recovering from homosexuality. Through this experience I discovered that my thinking was flawed. My abuse was by a man, so I thought that *all men* were abusers, and that they were never abused. I found out that the men in this group had also been abused by men or by *women. There were hurting little boys as much as there were hurting little girls.* When my little girl was able to identify with their little boys, the blanket of fear under which I had been hiding melted away. I did not have to run to women for relationships any longer. I believed *all men* were dangerous and would hurt me, but that was just not true. I could receive and enjoy the love of a good man. I just had to find one, and they did exist. This revelation was freeing for me, and I became a leader of this group.

The light began to shine on the little girl behind bars. The darkness was there, and in some places it was cloudy, but the light kept getting brighter and brighter! I was taught that God wanted me to behave according to His Word in all areas of my life. I realized that I was 'born-again' both spiritually and literally. **I'd been given another chance, a clean slate and a fresh start! What I had done before was not being held against me.** I had an immediate re-birth and the change was like day and night! So *I began to be transformed by changing my mind about all that I'd learned* if it disagreed with the Word of God. I found my new identity in Jesus Christ.

Eventually, I did so well on my job that I received a raise to $4.75 an hour. I was told that with my raise came cashiering responsibilities. I was petrified! This was the first real test of my "change" and I wasn't sure I would pass it. I took on the new responsibility and just willed myself to behave. I don't know how long it was after my promotion, but one day I was handling money and a sensation arose in my heart: I no longer had the desire to steal.

I was handling money that wasn't mine, and I was okay with it. I didn't want to steal it! You may not experience this the same way I did, you may have to discipline yourself by fleeing from temptation for years! There are some temptations I continue to resist.

During this time I was meeting people and learning how to be in good relationships. I met a man who seemed interested in me and we started dating. Interestingly enough, we met in the same circle of self-help groups. We were both in recovery! I'm sure you've noticed by now that: Hurting and unhealthy people draw hurting and unhealthy people; then they usually hurt each other.

Hurting and unhealthy people draw hurting and unhealthy people; then they usually hurt each other.

All the therapy and counseling prepared me to be productive and in control of my behaviors, but it did not teach me about dating. Things were going too fast, but I didn't know how to slow them down.

After coming out of such devastation, I really needed to know myself first. I didn't give myself that chance. I would caution anyone coming out of bondage, or even "healthy" people to invest time in getting to know *yourself* before dating and then to take things *very slowly.* We did not walk in wisdom. Instead, we married after only dating for six months. *Your feelings should not always be the motivation for your actions.* If you act on them, you will only end up where you were before. Feelings are valid, but they change. You don't want to make life-altering decisions solely on your feelings. Though I am still married ten years later, it has been difficult at times because we are still dealing with issues from which we didn't take the time to recover.

I would like to note that I have observed participants in *Having The Courage To Change* and other programs compound issues. Even though you're in recovery, you may not be as far along as you think you are. When you make a good choice and get a good response, you are encouraged to keep making better choices, but don't add more to your life than you can handle. If you say you're free, expect to be tested in that area.

The potential to steal, to deceive, to have addictive behaviors and relationships still lurks within me, but it is mastered and kept under control by the Spirit of God, *by the boundaries I set for myself,* and by the continual renewing of my mind. I don't allow myself to get too loose.

I believe it was only through God's intervention that my son's father heard about my wedding and decided to bring my son to see me get married. As I was putting on my dress, I turned around, and there was my beautiful son, nine years and eleven months old. I felt like I was being rewarded. The things that were taken from me were being restored. I was being put back together. It was my first semblance of having all of the parts of a family present. I now was a wife with a husband and a son. Of course, I did not count the cost of what all of this additional responsibility would mean to my recovery. It was going to pose some difficulty. Often we are unaware of the pressure adding even a good thing can present. We must be aware of ourselves: what we can and cannot take. I have seen many in recovery attempt to go on with their "regular lives" thinking that they can handle more than they really can.

I was certainly not exempt from testing. I had changed from a homosexual lifestyle and was now married. Tests and temptations came in every area I had overcome, *but my decision was to say, "NO!"* There was no struggle to avoid falling and failure, because *the "main" decision was made. I had decided to change my life.* It is so much easier to choose once you've settled your stance. A lot of people are in limbo. Few make the decision to change. I had been presented the choice to change five times before. Each time I'd made the wrong choice. Finally, after accepting Jesus Christ as my Savior, I received from God the ability to make right choices. My life has never been the same.

At the time, I needed to make more money, so I got a job in a health care facility for the elderly. I became a Certified Nursing Assistant making $7.80 an hour, full-time. I was disciplined with my money and began to save. I had never put value in money before, but now I was seeing it from a different perspective. My discipline in this area has been a testimony to others and I have had the opportunity to help causes and be a blessing. The ability to have more than enough in order to give is one of God's blessings.

One day I saw Les Brown, the motivational speaker, on TV and I knew that was what I wanted to do. So I just began to tell my story to anyone who would listen. A counselor asked if he could submit my story to the *Hamilton Journal*, a paper in the city where all my troubles began. That was certainly "coming full circle!" The name of the story was, "A Miracle on Front Street." Talbert House staff saw the story and asked me to volunteer leading groups and meetings. When they opened their new facility, they asked me to be the keynote speaker. I had been accustomed to sharing my testimony, but this was much different. They invited the three judges who were instrumental in my incarceration and release! *Instead of having to ask these judges for mercy, I now stood on equal footing with them and they were asking me for the benefit of* **my** *experience! My life had really changed!*

One day, I was on a bus going to a Women's Conference with my church. I was looking out the window when in my mind's eye I saw the words, *"Having The Courage To Change."* I saw group homes that would show women how to change their lives. I had a vision of a tunnel filled with darkness and nastiness. At the end of the tunnel there was a little light. God asked, "Will you help me?" I instantly said "no" because I knew how people really are! I was free and doing well for myself. At that time, I really had no desire to help anyone - I was just trying to help myself. I was self-absorbed as most of us are. I have learned now, that *freedom comes as you help others.*

After that bus trip from the Women's Conference, I went home and wrote fifteen pages of notes detailing what the ministry would do, whom it would serve and how it would operate. It just poured out of me like a bucket of water. I was so excited. It's amazing how a vision that comes from God just flows out of a vessel. It didn't matter that I was not already mature or in a place to see it implemented right then. This vision from God was powerful and began to set the course for the rest of my life. It still does today.

I cannot stress to you the importance of writing your vision down on paper. Where do you see yourself this year...in three to five years, and beyond? If you were addicted, will you be clean and sober? If you were homeless, what type of housing will you have?

What will you be doing? How will you look? How will your family life, career, and hobbies be? The prophet Habakkuk in the Bible was instructed by God to write down the vision he was receiving, to make it plain and understandable and post it so people who would see and hear it could make it happen; hence the term "run with the vision."

> *I cannot stress to you the importance of writing your vision down on paper.*

It's like a resume. You have an intention and qualifications. You word the intention in the part called: objective. "I am seeking a position in this field so that I will accomplish this goal or display this set of skills." Then you provide a history of experiences that qualify you to accomplish the task. My vision for **Having The Courage To Change** did the same thing. My objective was to see the lives of broken women changed by the power of the Gospel. My own life provided my qualifications. Once I began to tell my story, others joined with me to bring the vision to pass.

First, I submitted the vision to my local church. I thought the church might want to partner with me. They reviewed it for six months, offered to help, but were financially unable to do so. One of the Pastors suggested that it might not be for the church to do, that I may need to do it on my own. I decided I would. It is important to always allow things to flow. You may have in your mind the exact way you want things to work out, *"I'll be able to stay at this one's home...surely this relative will give me money...I know my friend will give me the hook up!"* I would suggest you write the vision of your deliverance and future goals and move without any pre-conceived notions. God may not choose to use the person you think He will use to help you and to bless you.

I spied out the land for a year. I did research and I prepared. Many people forget these steps when starting a new venture. They may have an idea, or even a vision statement, but they have not studied nor have they prepared in any way for the future. You have to act as if what you are conceiving is real. I had to see the women in my mind's eye, I had to see their clothing, shelter, housing, food, times of sharing and study. I had to visualize them changing their lives the same way I had changed mine.

I have spoken to many individuals and led many groups where people are confused about their purpose, calling and destiny. They wonder why they exist on the earth and what God's plan is for their lives. I firmly believe that part of what we are to do is tied up in our history. We are on the earth to help other people, but often our selfishness gets in the way. Every person in life who is successful is providing some sort of service. Doctors heal, garbage men collect our waste, teachers train minds, entertainers help us express emotion, preachers inspire us, business people create and distribute things that will make our lives easier, counselors help us heal, administrative assistants keep bosses together, and so on. What are you doing that helps someone else? What gifts have you been given that could be of service? What experiences do you have in life that could show someone else what to do or what not to do? Offer them to someone else. In giving away what you have, you gain a sense of connectedness with your fellow man. Paradoxically, our worth increases when we give away.

Application

~ What books or other materials have been an encouragement to you on your journey?

Chapter Eight

Restoration
A new beginning was about eight steps away...

In 1997, the same year that *Having The Courage To Change* opened, I attended our family reunion with my foster sister. There, I met a friend of my foster mother, Ms. Bernice. I soon found out she was not just an acquaintance of my foster mother's when she bluntly asked, *"Have you seen your mother?"*

I said, *"No,"* thinking she was referring to my dead foster mother, to which she replied,

*"No, your **real** mother. I saw her a couple of years ago. Her sister died of cancer. Your grandfather is a pastor who lives about three blocks down."*

I was stunned. I hesitated to reply. Ms. Bernice was both unaware of, and unconcerned with, the dynamics of my life and what this revelation might do to me. Since she had never been in my shoes, the significance of this type of meeting didn't move her at all. The liberty she took amazed me. Who was she to take control of this situation? She didn't really know me! How did she get to choose if and when I would meet my birth mother? I'd always thought I would go on a search when I felt led to do so. Ms. Bernice began to ask all sorts of private questions and I was not prepared to respond. All I could do was react. I didn't even get the opportunity to count the cost or decide what should be happening in this moment because it happened so quickly. Here was this stranger taking me on the most difficult journey of my life. If I'd had the chance to think about it, I probably would have thought myself out of meeting my birth mother, so I guess the suddenness was a good thing.

I had only dreamt about my real mother. I envisioned her to be a movie star or Tina Turner (since my name was Turner, too). I had rehearsed my fantasies about her so much that they became real to me. Would she be as I imagined or would I be devastated again to find out the truth? I had vowed in the cycle of self-protection that closely shadows the cycle self-abuse, that, *"I will not look for someone who has left me."*

So here was one more decision — another crossroads. To *maybe* know, *not* know, or *never* know. Which one was better? I decided that not knowing was the worst. So I drove the three blocks down the street to see my real grandfather. Perhaps he would be able to tell me where my mother was.

A grayhaired, frail man answered the door to an old and crumbling house that looked as ragged as he did. He did not have the look or demeanor of a pastor at all, but I guess that's where I inherited the call to ministry. He was as disinterested in me as Ms. Bernice was in my plight at her sudden revelation. I trembled as he opened the door and Ms. Bernice, who had just dropped the bombshell on me, asked him,

"Do you know where your daughter is?"

He said, *"Which daughter ya'll talkin' bout?"*

She replied, *"Evelyn."*

He answered, *"She lives right 'cross the street."*

It was about eight steps away.

Eight steps to make my dream come true; eight steps to the place where "not knowing" and "could know" would meet. *Eight steps that could change my life forever.*

I didn't know if I was ready. I could very easily envision a scenario of yet another abandonment, and I didn't want to face that. Fear gripped me so intensely that half of me wanted to jump into the car and ride away as fast as possible. The other half of me heard a voice saying, *"Fear not, I am with you, and nothing else in life can harm you."* There it was again, the same voice that had guided me out of the prison, led me to the Source of all things, and out of a life of self-abuse, was speaking to me about my destiny.

I believed that everything I needed to complete my life was across the street. The final chapter to a long history of miraculous occurrences would complete my history and really allow me to live was eight steps away. Isn't it funny how we often think that this next thing will finally satisfy us and once we get it, we believe that the thing after that will definitely complete us, until we want that other thing...well, anyway.

Eight steps to make my dream come true; eight steps to the place where "not knowing" and "could know" would meet. Eight steps that could change my life forever.

I walked past the car. *Each step was so heavy and intense because it was the unknown, which is often our greatest fear.* I had fantasized that my mother was Tina Turner. On August 3, 1997, I would find out the truth. That is, if she was at home.

I quickly found out that my mother was not Tina Turner, or anyone else rich or famous. *"My mother is poor!"*, I cried to myself in disbelief. Her house was as worn down as my newly-found grandfather's. I haven't inherited a thing! They can't help me. If anything, the person who lives in this house will be asking *me* for money! I juggled back and forth emotionally because I had always believed that my birth mother would bring fame and prosperity to me. My dreams of wealth shattered instantly, but the teeter of that totter was the spiritual significance of what meeting my mother would do and the gaps it might fill. There was great historical significance to me. So many questions would soon be answered. Still, my first thought was, *"This woman has nothing to offer me! What a waste!"*

Even though the outside did not look good, I was willing to go through with the meeting. My first impulse was to run and get back in the car, but I had become a person who faced life head on. I learned that I was no longer someone who would flee from challenges. As I stood on the front porch behind Ms. Bernice, the door opened and a skinny, frail, light-skinned woman with mid-length hair answered the door.

"*Hey, Evelyn,*" Ms. Bernice said, "*Do you remember me?*"

My mother said, "*No.*"

Not, "*Come on in child, how you been all these years!*" Just, "*No.*"

"*Oh my God,*" I thought, "*She doesn't even know Ms. Bernice! If she can't even recognize her long lost friend, she definitely won't know who I am!*" I thought to myself, "*I'm about to really be embarrassed.*" I was angry. Ms. Bernice had taken me through this emotional trauma, and I distrusted that anything significant would come from it.

"*Evelyn, I used to work at the dry cleaners on 22nd Street with you,*" she explained.

"*Yah,*" my mother replied. She didn't speak English well, just "yah, uh uhm, dat, etc.," and she had a fiery attitude. She seemed annoyed at the whole process. Evelyn was stubborn and angry, which unfortunately reminded me of my old self. At least there was a crack of a door open, since she knew she'd worked at the cleaners and was still listening to Bernice's tale.

Bernice went on to ask, "*Do you know who this is?*"

My mother replied, "*Is that your daughter?*"

"*No*", she replied, "*I think it's your daughter.*"

"*My daughter is Dolly,*" my mother stated emphatically.

"*No, this is your daughter Lucretia.*"

"*No,*" my mother corrected her, "*I have a daughter named Lucreta.*" Like she hadn't just said she only had a daughter named Dolly a few seconds ago.

"*Lucreta!*" I thought. I might have been calling myself by the wrong name for all my life!

She turned to me and asked, "*Who are you and when were you born?*"

"September 12, 1960," I replied.

"That's the day of my daughter's birth, but where were you born?"

"In Louisville, Kentucky, to an Evelyn Weaver Turner."

"Okay," she said, and we were invited into the house as she went upstairs.

Ms. Turner went to get the birth certificate of *Lucreta*. I was still attempting to embrace this new name that I'd heard for the first time. I happened to have a wallet size copy of my birth certificate with me. I showed her my birth certificate and asked if it was the same.

She reluctantly said, *"Oh, okay then. I guess you are my daughter."*

I was her daughter! Relief! I finally know who I am, and where I came from. Even if I don't like it, at least I know. The pieces of my life's puzzle were finally coming together. I looked into her eyes longing for the same response, but there was nothing in them but a blank stare and a look of resignation. My heart reached for the sound that comes with a connection, but her lack of emotion was screaming louder to me than my excitement at finding her. Then she gave me what felt like an obligatory hug, since I was her daughter, but it was empty, like swinging your arms around just to hold air.

Evelyn Turner's son, Phillip, was on the porch when all this was happening. I knew from experience that he was geeked out on crack cocaine. He was shocked and exclaimed,

"I don't believe this! This doesn't happen to real people! This is like Jerry Springer!"

He began to ask his mother questions about his new-found sister.

"What happened? Why didn't you tell us anything about her?"

He was immediately scolded, *"This is none of your business!"*

To which he grumbled, *"It's my sister."*

My new-found brother asked me things like, *"Who kept you all those years?"*

I recounted to him the story that I had been told about Ms. Turner giving me up to my foster mother.

"*I never gave you to her,*" she countered, "*she kidnapped you! I asked her to watch you for a couple of hours, and she took you away.*"

I did not indulge in the possibility of this scandalous story since my foster mother was now dead and I was at peace with her memory. I respectfully asked Ms. Turner not to taint that memory, but to keep it as precious as possible by not sharing this story. In addition to my new-found sister and brother, I learned that I also had a brother in prison. I finally met him at my birth mother's funeral. I was hurt that I had been the only child who was not kept and raised by my mother, and I wondered why. But it would later be revealed that Ms. Turner didn't really raise any of her children. Their grandmother had raised them. We had all been abandoned, and it didn't surprise me that we ended up in prison and on drugs. The abandonment and abuse had left us little boys and girls

We live out of our imagination because it is easier to do that than face reality, or we mask and medicate ourselves with substances, lies, relationships — whatever will temporarily make the pain of truth go away.

incarcerated behind the barbed wire of shame and rejection.

We invited Evelyn to the cookout and she went dutifully. She met my foster family and my husband and son. My foster sister remembered some of the background of my birth family. She had gotten the names mixed up and believed that Dolly was my mother, but she was really my sister.

I was overwhelmed and shocked at all that had been discovered, and numbed by my birth mother's mindset, her wall of distance and her continual denial about giving me up. I was disappointed at the fact that after all these years, she was not waiting with bated breath for me, nor did she embrace me with open arms.

I soon realized that she had nothing to give me, spiritually, naturally, financially or emotionally. Only a new name: *Lucreta*.

Often, those who begin to journey along the cycle of self-abuse have an unresolved relationship or issue from childhood. We find ourselves doing so many things to make up for what was lost. We manipulate our minds to come up with conclusions, reasons and rationalizations for why things transpired the way they did.

We live out of our imagination because it is easier to do that than face reality, like, *"My mom had to go on tour with the band, so she left me with a friend and said she'll be back soon."* or we mask and medicate ourselves with substances, lies, relationships – whatever will temporarily make the pain of truth go away.

When the illusions that we conjure up are finally faced with the truth, we don't know how to handle it. We can no longer run into the cave of denial. We must now accept that we can't rely on the fantasy of what we thought should be, nor prop ourselves up on self-abusive crutches any longer.

What we really need, God has placed inside us from the beginning. It is the yearning for healing inside of us that leads us back to our Creator – the only one who can soothe our emotions and heal our pain. *Even if our parents, spouses, children could give explanations - they wouldn't be enough.* Even if relationships could be restored, there would still be losses to grieve of time and opportunity. Even if they were as good as they could be to us now, it would not recover for us the sense of self-esteem and love that we were always looking for in the eyes of others – but never quite seemed to see when we looked in the mirror.

On September 12th, my birthday, I received my first letter from my mother along with $20.00! I thought, *"She really accepts me now!"* In December, my husband and I went to visit her for a weekend. I began to ask her all sorts of questions, but I found myself knocking my head against a brick wall. She was only going to go so far, only going to get so close, particularly when I questioned her about the sore subject of this so-called *"kidnapping." "Why didn't you come after me? You could have called the police!"* To which she replied, *"I left you with her and when I came back from work, she was gone." "Well, how long did yo leave me? Did you search for me?"* Vague, nondescript answers formed a wall. I knew she was lying.

At this point there was a perfect opportunity for the same issues of abandonment, rejection, and insecurity to creep up in my life. *I could have relapsed and lost everything that I had worked so hard to rebuild in my life.* I was devastated! I couldn't get what I wanted from my mother.

I would never see the approval and acceptance I wanted in her eyes, but, boy, did I try! For three years off and on I maintained a relationship with her. I traveled to see her, at times with my family and friends.

I kept seeking in her what I already had inside of me. I already had more than enough love, life, inner joy and peace.

Even the simple things I sought, like answers to questions about my health history were elusive. My excitement and expectations were greatly disappointed. Again, one day, I heard the voice say, *"You will never have definition or meaning until you return to the Source. I never sent you back to get what you wanted, but what I wanted you to have."*

I knew what that meant. Earlier on in April of 1997, I had an impression from God that I would receive a new name. Four months later, I found my birth mother and discovered that my name was Lucreta, not Lucretia. It was Evelyn Turner's role to reveal my new name: nothing more, nothing less. I sought and pursued her for a validation that she wasn't ever meant to give. I had already received validation from God.

It is amazing how we chase after things and people to give us worth and to validate our existence in the world. We say to ourselves, *"I'll be worth something if I have this, or if I get in this relationship."* Wherever you go, you're still there. *If you're miserable and unfulfilled alone, be sure that you'll still be that way, even surrounded by all the people and things you ever wanted.*

Evelyn Turner became ill and went into the hospital while I was on a trip to Florida. I was told that I would be informed of her condition and I decided I would see her when I returned. I returned on Sunday, September 25, 2000. On Monday the 26th, my sister called to say that Evelyn Turner was dead.

I had mixed feelings because of my unresolved issues. I felt not only a sense of loss of the relationship that was, but the one that could have been. I was disappointed. I was hurt. *I had really set myself up for failure.* We are disappointed by our own expectations and frustrated by our own fantasies. I once heard a man say that...

Great problem-solvers realize what they have and what they want, and in between the two is the problem they must solve.

At the funeral, I had to finally accept, after three years of trying, that I would never have what I wanted out of that

The only limitations you have are those in your own mind.

relationship. The exclamation point on that truth was the fact that *I was not even mentioned as Evelyn Turner's daughter in the obituary.*

She was never meant to mother me. She was just the vehicle God used to get me here, and she was the one who would give me my new name. You see, the change of name alone meant a new identity for me. Lucreta had never been abused. She had never stolen anything nor been in jail. She had never lived a lesbian lifestyle, nor had several miscarriages. Lucreta was new to me. She allowed me to kick the dirt of Lucretia off.

Lucretia was a thief, a drug abuser, and an inmate. She was abrasive and harsh, not feminine. She was full of pain. Lucretia was my old person. But who was I supposed to be now? How would Lucreta live? I felt like a little girl getting a new identity.

This is the joy of the "born again" experience, a tenet of the Christian faith. A person can come to God as an evil or sinful person and upon believing in Christ to save them, receive a new identity, a new nature, new beliefs, new behaviors, new positive consequences, and a new life! They are restored to a state of innocence, just like I was given a new name to go with my birth certificate. I was reborn and able to re-learn how to live as Lucreta and not Lucretia!

Wouldn't you love the opportunity to start all over again and get a different result? I have, and I assure you that it can be done!

On October 5, 2000, a week after my mother's death — my new-found brother Phillip, died of a massive heart attack. Unlike my mother, Phillip accepted me from the start and embraced me as part of the family. In fact, I said a few words at his committal, and I was listed as his sister in the obituary. God can restore what has been lost through simple expressions of His love. Now I had four families: my immediate family (husband and son), my foster family, my birth family and the family of God into which I had been born again and accepted! God loved me so much that he gave me quadruple the families I had initially!

Application

~ Are you so close to your new beginning, yet so far away, because of fear?

Chapter Nine

Since I've Changed...

I have told you the basics of my life story up until recent years. Some of the history of the ministry of **Having The Courage To Change** will come in subsequent pages. I outlined my struggles so that you would have hope. If God can change someone who has been exposed to as much hurt and abuse as I have (even the self-inflicted abuse), surely you are not beyond help!

You might ask, *"Lucreta, what has happened in your life recently?"* I assure you that my life has not been without challenges, growth and struggle. Thanks to God and a lot of hard work, I have a healthy marriage of over 10 years. We have laughed, fought, cried and worked together. We've been in marital and family counseling to help us heal the wounds of the past. I can say that our life together is sweeter and more joyful than ever. I love my husband tremendously and am grateful for his support.

My son is now in college and I am extremely proud of him. Our relationship has been restored and we are very close. I am grateful to have the honor of motherhood in his adult years.

As my story became known throughout the Tri-State Area (Ohio, Indiana and Kentucky), I was sought after to give my testimony at churches. I have become a licensed minister with my home church and with City Ministries, **Having The Courage To Change's** partner and sponsor. I speak about my life and teach about the process of change as a trainer in correctional facilities, halfway houses and other recovery programs. I am a mentor to men and women who are committed to changing their lives.

These opportunities have caused me to become a community leader. I received an "Image Maker" award in the City of Cincinnati 1996. My story and experience also garnered attention on a national level when I appeared as a counselor on the *Maury Povich Show* in 1995.

I remain free because I continue to grow in my relationship and fellowship with my Lord and Savior Jesus Christ. I revere God. I surround myself with like-minded people who yearn for change and development. I meditate and pray for others as well as for myself. I study the Bible and other books that continue to assist me in the process of change. I live honestly and am not in denial about my choices. I face the consequences of my decisions and I realize that my choices affect others, not just myself. Before I take on any endeavor, I count the cost to see if I can do it. I want to be upheld in my integrity.

I have learned that I not only have gifts, but I am a gift. I have something to pour out to others that is valuable, that has delivered me and can do the same for others also. I have learned to love myself and to treat myself well, rather than abuse myself. In learning to love God and myself, I can now treat my neighbor right. I have a godly "want to." I want to change. I want to be whole.

I take steps of faith to believe and see restoration and wholeness in my life. To the reader I would say that restoration is inside of you. It will take hard work for you to realize it and begin to pursue it. You don't need other people to be validated and restored to peace, joy, health and well being, but you do need God. You with God is more than enough!

Application

~ Are there gifts inside of you that have been discovered since you've been in the process of change? If so, list them.

Award nomination salutes courage to change

By Al Salvato
POST STAFF REPORTER

Five years ago, Lucretia Turner Bowman sat in jail, dreaming of the man she could be the person she is today.

She swore to shed her criminal ties and vowed to help other women better their lives. She is quietly working to make a mark on this world.

Two judges believed her and helped her leave prison early. She toured a job program who trusted in her. This

Celebrating the 'Miracle on Front Street'

By Jeff Hannon
SPECIAL FROM

'My greatest pride is being someone who knows where I came from and where I am today.'

Lucretia Turner Bowman

Mt. Auburn homes offer women hope

Many find life worth living now

By Jeff Louden
POST STAFF REPORTER

Lucretia Bowman in the kitchen of the new home for women in Mt. Auburn.

Incarceration mixed with care

72-bed facility in Warren County is halfway house, prison

BY TANYA BRICKING

These are [ ] the cheapest of programs to operate, but if they can demonstrate that they're reducing subsequent criminal behavior . . . then certainly they cost-effectiveness.

— Edward Latessa, UC professor

Career criminal: 'You can change'

God, will and judges turned her life around

By Al Salvato
POST HISTORIAN

Lucretia Turner Bowman with the story of today's visitor

Section Two:

Do You
Have The Courage
To Change?

⊱┈◈┈○┈◈┈⊰

Dear Honorable Valen;

I'm writing you in concern of the motion for Shock Probation that has been presented to you, in my interest. As you already know, I've been incarcerated for 7 months here at the Ohio Reformatory for Women, during this most valuable period of my life, I've experienced alot of situations, that before in my life I took for granted. Some small; some big; but both being very important to how one should maintain themselves in order to live a productive life outside in the community.

Upon my arrival here at the Institution I went through a rough time adjusting to my surroundings, which was a big disadvantage to my health. Through that most depressing event, with help from the "Good Lord" as well as good "Doctor's" I survived, only to really. I won it!! here; had to

Chapter Ten

After these horrible events occurred in my life,
I began to abuse myself.

I have defined self-abuse as: *treating yourself improperly, insulting or reviling (hating) yourself; bringing yourself into perversion.* It is the negative response or reaction you have to adverse circumstances that manifest in self-injury. We abuse ourselves all of the time, but we don't realize it. It is the one thing in our lives we can really change.

Have you experienced the ebb and flow of the cycle of self-abuse?

Initially, the tragic event occurs. Many experience this like I did in childhood. It is not normal for a child to be abandoned, rejected, molested, shaken or beaten beyond recognition, malnourished, verbally assaulted, impoverished, put in an institution, etc. But it happens far too often. Children were meant to be able to trust the adults in their environment; they are to be protected. In our culture we have lost sight of this awesome responsibility. If you have a child or are around one, please take the task very seriously. The molding and shaping of their life is literally in your hands!

Even in youth or adulthood an event can take place that shakes your very foundation. It could be a rape or assault, loss of a child, close family or friend, witnessing a crime, an illness or loss of mobility, infidelity or a divorce, loss of career or any event that you feel is devastating to your core being. These types of events can do several things to our psyche:

1. They can cause us to question our worth and identity.
2. They can bring insecurity where there was once trust.

3. They can cause us to have a distorted perception of ourselves and the meaning of the event.

I say "can" because often through proper handling of a tragic situation you might see one person flourish and do well, while another embarks on the cycle of self-abuse. After I was abandoned and abused, I no longer trusted any adult in authority. Now that I look back, though I said I did, I also did not trust myself. As I stated earlier, a child thinks that everything that happens to him/her was their fault. So if something bad has happened, I must be bad. Surely no one who was really worth anything would have had this happen!

This can happen to adults as well. The rape victim is questioned about what clothes she was wearing, as if it was her fault that she was violently attacked. We begin to identify ourselves as victims and as "the abused." *We become the incident, rather than a survivor of it.* We identify with our hurt more than we do our strength. But we have made it through and continue to live! We think that this event means we are horrible, ugly, worthless, and should be full of shame. In reality, we are wonderful, beautiful, of infinite worth and have nothing to be ashamed about. I challenge you to look at what you're really made of. Many people could not have survived what you've been through, but you're still here and on the way to changing your life forever!

Many psychologists say that you must trust yourself before you can trust others. You must trust that you can make it through whatever individuals might say or do to you in order for you to live freely. The Bible states, *"the fear of man brings a snare."* We are held hostage by this fear all the time. *"If they leave me, I don't know what I'd do."* Yes, you do! You'd continue to live! We must believe that if they hit us, *we will leave,* because we are worth more than being hit. If they laugh and talk about us, we will rise above that because we mean more than what others think of us. If we find ourselves broke, we will find a way to rise from the ashes because we have more than enough faith, strength, wisdom and opportunity. We are not ignoring the root of the problem. If we need counseling, we get it. If we must face ourselves by journaling every day and reading self-help books, we do it. We do not respond to the initial event any more by ignoring it or temporarily medicating it! We face it and deal with it! This is how you break the cycle in the very beginning.

"Well, Lucreta, I didn't break it. I didn't ignore the root problem and I did medicate it. Time passed, I thought everything was all right and I was handling it. But I really wasn't."

I understand, you went through the cycle like I did:

1. You confirmed your false reality and made it more true with each event.
2. You built walls around yourself because of a lack of trust.
3. You exercised flight-or-fight and began to experience the consequences of your choice in your body, mind and situations.

I have found in my recovery that half of the battle toward freedom is studying myself. Why did I do certain things? What was I thinking? My pastor taught a sermon on **The Five Whys.** He stated that when you look at a situation or your response to it, you should go down through five levels of why.

- I am stealing. Why?
- Because I have to get things for myself. Why?
- Because I don't trust anyone else to do it for me. Why?
- Because no one takes care of me. Why?
- Because they really can't take care of themselves. Why?
- Because they're hurt just like me and never had anyone to care for them as a child.

Go down as many "whys" as you need to so that you can get to the truth of the matter.

If you don't, you will confirm in your mind that everyone is against you, out to hurt you, can't be trusted. You will continue to be the little girl/boy or grown woman/man behind bars. You will have locked yourself into a prison from which only you can free yourself. You will abuse your own imagination, rehashing the events, and simulating in your mind different outcomes. You might even create a new imaginary world for yourself and live there more than in reality. The unreal can become more real than the truth through the flawed lens of your mind's eye. That is until you face the truth. Facing the truth is key to breaking the cycle.

You will run from or fight situations and people rather than face yourself and use critical thinking, good reasoning and self-control to see the truth and walk in it. Running from a situation is not just literal. Some people avoid things and exist in their shell as a form of running. Some fight and control others with a passive aggressive silence, or other covert tactics. As I said before, hurting people hurt people. It is only in compassion that we can break part of the cycle by seeing that our abusers are hurting people and forgiving them, as Jesus said, *"for they know not what they do."*

Unfortunately, many people would rather live inside a prison of unforgiveness, mentally captive to their memories. They are emotionally paralyzed over events that occurred long ago. They want so badly to be free of the offender, but they've attached themselves to them and are now co-dependent on them and the event for survival. They identify more with that than anything else in their life.

This is the worst kind of prison, because not only are you locked up, but you are eating away at your own life and body. Forgiveness is meant to release YOU even if it does nothing for your abuser. It frees YOU from the anger, grudge-holding, and the desire to retaliate that have embittered you for years. Forgiveness relieves stress-related conditions like: high blood pressure, ulcers, cancer, migraines and heart conditions. Forgiving the one who hurt you and forgiving yourself will break the cycle of self-abuse! If not, you are sentencing yourself to life in prison — your own death row!

I would like to submit to you that the cycle (illustrated at the end of this chapter) can be broken at different points. You can forgive yourself and your abuser first, or you can face the truth first. All of these can be "breaking points." If you don't break the cycle, you will:

1. Begin a chain reaction of events that exacerbate further abusing yourself.
2. Create a lifestyle of "CONTROL."
3. Become the abuser.

After a time of reacting to your tragedy and abusing yourself, you can become so sure about self-abuse and your skills in the world of your own prison, that you begin to want incarceration and accept addiction! Then you begin to set up controls to preserve the 'safety and security' of your abusive lifestyle! I used my body to control men. I stole to "create my own security." I had a child to try to ensure that I would be loved. I had simulated "families" in prison. Incarceration seemed more normal to me than "free" life.

Eventually, after becoming so used to being abused and abusing ourselves, many go on to abuse others. We may not think that stealing, having multiple sex partners, cheating on our taxes, etc., is abusing someone else, but it is! There is a victim to every abuse. Don't victimize yourself or others!

Finally, some people like myself go through almost the entire cycle. They hit rock bottom and have to have a moment of divine inspiration directly from God. At this "Aha" moment of self-awakening, a light shines on you. You realize now by God's grace that you have been locked in that prison and you desperately want to get out:

1. You acknowledge and are grateful for Divine providence.
2. You experience an awakening to your true incarcerated self.
3. You begin to see the new person you can become.
4. You realize that quality decision-making is needed in your life.
5. You seek out help to change.
6. You begin to set boundaries.
7. You make steps to change, acting on decisions and advice.
8. You embark upon your new life, while you are still changing!

There are so many people I know who, like myself, had

destroyed their lives, their familial relationships and, in their minds, any hope of change. They were in the gutter, but supernaturally God called them out of the pit they were in and changed their lives completely! It has happened to me, and it can happen to you.

When I saw that I was the little girl, I was stunned. I had not realized what I had done to myself. As soon as I did, I began to take steps toward freedom. I was not going to let anyone or anything stop me from being free!

I began to seek out wise and godly counsel wherever I could find it. I was desperate for change. If it meant I had to monitor every move I made, I was going to do it! I went to therapists. I went to church. I asked friends to hold me accountable.

I set boundaries. There were places that I would no longer go, people with whom I could no longer associate. How could I change if I were constantly around the same influences and incarcerated mindsets? In order for any of us to change, we must change our internal thinking, and our outward behaviors and manifestations. Yes, a former lesbian will have to change how she acts, thinks and even dresses to move to a heterosexual state. A former drug addict or alcoholic will have to cease interactions with drugs, drug paraphernalia, and other addicts. A gossip will have to get off the phone with other gossips, and stop making appointments to talk about people. It costs to change!

As long as we live, we will be changing, making adjustments and going on with life. I don't know where you are in your cycle of self-abuse, but I'm sure you're at a place where you can break it!

A Cycle of Self-Abuse

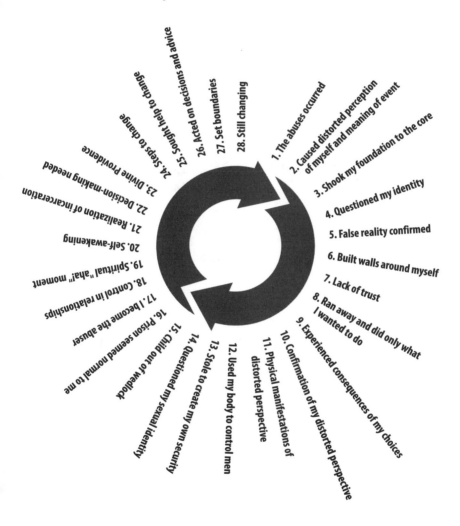

The Courage to Change

Lucretia Turner Bowman grew up behind bars. A runaway at age 12, Lucretia called state institutions and prisons "home" for the next 20 years of her life.

"Every crime I was accused of, I committed," she admits today. In 1990, she decided it was time to try something different. From her prison cell, she wrote a letter asking her sentencing judge for another chance.

"I told him I didn't know how to live, but I was willing to learn how to live," Lucretia remembers.

At Talbert House for Women, Lucretia began the painful process of rebuilding her life. First, she faced the "dark places" in her past: abandonment by her birth mother and years of sexual abuse at the hands of an older neighbor.

"Those things had become crutches, and once I faced them, I didn't need those crutches anymore. I could walk on my own," she says.

Next, she wrote goals for

Lucretia Turner Bowman: "I didn't know how to live, but I was willing to learn . . ."

herself, developing a plan of action.

"Without a plan of action, you have no direction, and without direction, you get lost," she explains.

Three years out of the program, Lucretia owns a home, is happily married, and works as a motivational speaker, bringing her message to others in need.

"Talbert House for Women was such a foundation for my recov-

ery," she tells women in the program today. "This place and this staff is not here to babysit you, but to let you take action in your life. . . .

"Fear, and other people's opinions of us, keep a lot of us in a place we don't want to be. But you don't have to let other people's opinion of you become your reality. And if you participate in your life, you can be whatever you want."

A decision that made a difference

Lucretia credits Butler County Common Pleas Court Judge Anthony Valen and Hamilton County Common Pleas Court Judge Norbert Nadel with giving her the chance to change.

After carefully considering Lucretia's request, the two judges concurred in a decision to move her from a state prison to Talbert House for Women, where she says she found the foundation for her recovery.

<u>Judge Valen:</u>

"There was something in her letters and her attitude that made me feel she was ready."

<u>Judge Nadel:</u>

"Community corrections programs work if the person is motivated, and we're always happy to hear success stories."

Chapter Eleven

A model for change

My pastor recently shared with us the difference between Technical Change and Adaptive Change. When you change Technically, you're just "patch-working" behaviors *(usually to please others)* that make it look like you've made a real change. There is no inward work, just an outward show. This type of change is not lasting, but it's easier in the short-run. Adaptive Change works at the core of who you are, by changing the inward beliefs and attitudes that produce behavior.

Adaptive Change is more difficult, usually takes longer and can be more costly, but in the long run it yields lasting and permanent rewards in quality of life. It is a true change, made with wisdom and the God-assisted will to live in victory over your past, your personal demons and your own selfishness. You must have courage to face your fears and change in this way.

The following is the step model of Adaptive Change for *Having The Courage To Change:*

STEP 1 **After trying all that you know to do, come to the end of yourself and surrender to God.**

It was after I listened to the voice that spoke to me that I, *"would not find fulfillment and meaning in my life until I returned to the Source,"* that my life began to change. I could not change on my own; I needed Someone higher and stronger than myself. They tell you this in most 12-Step programs. I identified my Source as the Lord Jesus Christ, without whom I can do nothing and am nothing.

STEP 2 Accept the fact that through God you can be restored to wholeness.

It is a fact that we all can be restored to wholeness through the power of God. I've heard many who don't believe in Him say that they are sure that if they just followed His precepts and walked by the instruction of the Bible, their lives would be better. I believe this is the truth. The question is, will *you* accept it as truth? You must make that decision for yourself. You cannot rely on the faith of your father, mother or grandmother. Because we live in a society that promotes "looking out for number one" and "taking care of yourself," we often neglect our need for and allegiance to God. Then we are unwilling, unable or fearful of letting ourselves go, in order to trust that through Him we can recover our true selves. I knew of God for many years, had even heard His voice, but I had to believe that He would help me and heal me.

STEP 3 Turn your life over to God and walk through the process.

Unfortunately, people are looking for a zap. One of our pastors says we stand in front of the microwave yelling for it to "hurry up" and give us our food. We want "microwave" healing, deliverance and restoration, and if the microwave could go faster, we would want that. There is no "drive-thru deliverance!" It did not take you five minutes, five days or even five weeks to get into the mess you're in, so it certainly may take some time to get out.

It is a process to leave our old lives. It's work to change our minds from our former thought patterns. It's often difficult to leave friends and family behind or to deal with their perceptions about your change. However, all of this is necessary to go through the process of change. That takes a surrendered, flexible life that is not angry at or struggling with God.

STEP 4 Go back into the dark places of your life with God and turn on the light of truth.

This is one of the most difficult things you can attempt. It is the place where your mind and emotions have shut down to the degree that your decision-making becomes skewed. It's where wrong is right and right is wrong, and confusion abounds. It's also where an event has occurred (often in childhood) that is so painful that we don't want to feel it again. We put it away somewhere in a box, compartmentalizing it, so we don't have to open up the drawer to our hurt and pain.

As it only takes a small fire of a candle to bring light to a completely darkened and locked room, so a small amount of the light of God can enable us to see in places of our lives where we have been groping around blindly, so that we can find the doorway that will lead us out into freedom. My reaction to three dark childhood experiences caused me to lose years of my life. Not just the years when the events occurred, but all of the years I spent reacting, avoiding and acting out. My first impulse was to run from the pain and from what I had become. Until I realized that the only way out is THROUGH the pain, I was still stuck in the life of self-abuse and self-fulfilling prophecies.

STEP 5 Confess your faults to yourself, to God and others, and then turn around and begin to change.

First, we have to acknowledge that anything we have thought or done, omitted or committed, that was against the standards of God, is sin or missing God's mark. Everyone has sinned, so that probably makes things a whole lot easier. If you say you haven't done anything wrong, you're in denial and lying to yourself. "I didn't mean to," "I'm really a nice person" and "other people have done worse," are all excuses for not owning up to the responsibility and consequences of our actions. Of course, this has become a very popular thing to do in our culture.

Once you are ready to own up and be accountable to yourself, to God and others through confession, there will be a sense of freedom. But wait! You're not totally out of the woods yet. You must repent or turn away from your thought patterns, attitudes and behaviors to really experience victory. Repent also means to think at the top again. The suffix "pent" is in "penthouse." God's intention is that you recover and regain His standard, your innocence and a positive outlook, and live out the highest and best life He has to offer you. When I wrote the letter to the judge, I had to be open and honest about myself. This literally opened the door to my freedom, and I have been walking by this standard ever since. People may not always like what I'm saying or how I'm saying it, but they know I'm being truthful to God and myself.

STEP 6

Recognize the destructive behaviors inherent in the cycle of self-abuse.

It is difficult to see that you have a stronghold, a fortress that keeps you locked up inside. It could be a behavior that puts you on a merry-go-round of misery, or a thought pattern that causes a type of insanity — doing the same thing over and over and expecting a different result. It may help you to ask a trusted friend or confidant what they see in you if you have difficulty identifying areas that require attention. The wounds of a friend are faithful, but the kisses of an enemy are deceitful. No longer allow others to lie to you about yourself, to "call you out of your name" or your new-found freedom. Most of all don't lie to yourself! Denial is such a stronghold for the abused and addicted. There was a time when I knew that stealing was a stronghold for me. So I did not put myself in a tempting situation until I knew that stronghold had been broken in my life.

STEP 7

Walk humbly before God. Allow your humility to help you see those you have negatively affected.

You may have heard the proverb, "pride goes before destruction and a haughty spirit before a fall." Humility before God and with others is the surest way to receive any kind of help. Did you know that God actually resists people who are proud, but gives His grace (unmerited favor and divine ability) to those who are humble? As we admit our weakness to God, we place ourselves in a position to receive His strength. At first, I thought I knew everything, especially about handling my life. All that I'd really known was how to react to and survive in adversity. I didn't know how to live and thrive. I was unaware that my act wasn't fooling anyone, especially not God. He will use situations to bring you low, so that you can look up to Him and LIVE!

Once you are really walking on your path to wholeness it may be a good idea to speak directly to those who were affected by your previous behavior. Sometimes the person you wish to see has passed away or is unavailable to you for another reason. In this case, speak to them as if they were sitting in a chair across from you, or write them a letter to help to resolve your feelings. Confession, as they say, "is good for the soul."

However, if the people you affected are influences that may lead you back into negative behaviors, this may not be the best thing. It can be good to allow others who may have been negatively affected by your behavior to see that there is a new you. If they find it hard to believe you and trust you again, be understanding. Even you may not have grown to the point of trusting yourself yet! If they receive you, know that it is a test of the new standard that you are setting for your life. Let them know that you may not behave perfectly from now on, but you have made a determination to value yourself and others and LIVE! A healing in my life took place when I was able to reunite with my foster mother through a letter, and especially with my son.

STEP 8   **Receive God's wisdom when confessing or making amends to those you have affected and take daily inventory so that when you fall short, you learn to confess and repair breaches immediately.**

Twelve-step programs will tell you to make apologies or amends to those whom you have hurt. Situations exist where apologies can and should be made or items that have been stolen can be returned. We must receive God's wisdom about restitution; sometimes it is impossible to repay what has been taken away and only God Himself can comfort and repay the other individual. As much as I could, I have confessed to those my sins have affected and I still do. In fact, this book is a kind of confession. My desire is that I be free of any possible condemnation, that there be no place where I could be held hostage over what I have or have not done.

As I have stated time and time again, this is a PROCESS and a JOURNEY. When you are old and gray, there will still be areas in your behavior, attitude and thought life that will need tweaking. We need to look at life like a marathon rather than a sprint. Each and every step on this long journey leads to the finish line. *If I stop at 3 miles, 5 miles, 15 miles or even 25.29 miles — I have not completed the race!* In order to win, we must train ourselves to work on ourselves, particularly on our inward selves. We may slow down, we may even have to stop and be refreshed, but the intention is to finish the race and endure to the end. Don't allow yourself to wallow in temporary conditions that slow you down. Don't let yourself lie there when you fall. Admit your mistake, dust yourself off, and get back in the race of life! If I had quit every time I stumbled, I would not have been qualified to help other women or write this book!

STEP 9   Pray, meditate on, and study the Word of God.

It is amazing to me how many people do not pray. They complain to God, they worry in front of God, but they don't ever ask Him for anything specific. I guess they don't believe He hears. I assure you, God hears and answers prayer. He may say "No" or "Wait," but He definitely hears and answers. Prayer entails a dialogue with God. We talk — He hears and answers; He talks — we hear and obey. How do we hear the voice of God? He put His intentions in a letter to us called the Bible.

If you never heard an audible voice in your head like I did, that would not excuse you for not knowing how to live. That's why the Bible was written! It is, as one pastor says, "God's Manual for Life." When you receive the Bureau of Motor Vehicle's manual to get your license, you read it, study it, even memorize it for the test that you have to pass to be allowed to drive. To be allowed to live properly, we must read the Bible, think about it, study it — even memorize it — to be ready for the tests of life. Then, just as you actually *use* the guidelines in the motor vehicle manual when you drive, you use Biblical precepts as you live. If you ignore or disobey the guidelines of either manual, you are in violation. You are accountable for *all* of what's in the book, whether you read it or not. The policeman is still going to give you a citation. Man does not live by bread alone. We live by the Word of God. There is a consistent flowing-out of discipline, instruction, revelation, wisdom, knowledge and understanding. God has given us in His Word a steady stream of instructions that will assist us with the daily situations we face – if we'll just get in the book!

STEP 10 You are equipped. Now go back and strengthen others.

Why has all this happened to me? Why did I have to go through this? Why was I allowed to survive it? Is there any "purpose or meaning" to my life? I've heard it said that your misery is your ministry. Once you have been changed, your responsibility is to strengthen others. So many people have no hope and are in need of an example: a living, breathing testimony that you can do it by the grace and the goodness of God. It takes an unselfish person to be willing to lay down his/her life, to confess his/her faults, to help another up step-by-step, and to catch them when they fall. This is what Christ my Savior did for me. This is what I was meant to do in the lives of women and men across this country and in the world. It is why I have come through what I am sharing with you.

Who I am and where I have been is uniquely tied to my destiny. God gave me the opportunity to serve others, to teach them how to change. Are you willing to unselfishly abandon your independence and self-will for someone else's sake? What if it were just for your children, your family members and friends? People are waiting, watching and hoping for someone like you to *Have the Courage to Change!*

I have shared with you the course of my life, my experiences and my point of change. When I developed *Having The Courage To Change* I developed these steps to make it easier for others to follow. *Helping others has helped me to recover and has made me personally accountable.* I do not want to have preached to and taught others and find myself in their same predicament. Therefore, I am, as you will always be, still in the process of discovering myself.

The Prayer of Change

God, Help me to begin the process of change, by being willing to admit and accept my present condition...
God, Give me the courage to wait for You to renew my strength...
God, Lift me up and encourage me to see the storms and situations of my life from an eagle's viewpoint. The higher You lift me, the smaller they become...
God, Make me able to run and not become weary, to walk through my change and not faint, give up, cave in, or quit. Amen!

As we journey through the sometimes difficult process of change, God often graces us with creative outlets that reveal our true selves and stimulate our imaginations to soar to heights and joys we have never known. Some engage in temporary retreats to far-off lands by reading or writing books, others are transported to emotional healing by music that soothes the soul. Some are fascinated by technical concepts or philosophies that challenge them to think beyond what they see. Still others release stresses and exude positive energies by movement and dance. Whatever your outlet may be, I challenge you to absorb or express yourself creatively, as part of the process of change. It doesn't matter if you do it well, only that you do it. Play at it like you did as a child. Let it bring you joy, and don't be surprised if you find yourself being freed along the way! Sudden problems in my life usually indicate a need to work on my art.

Julia Cameron

Why Won't You Dance?

Broken heart, consumed mind
Where lies your dignity?
You sit with your head down
And emotions bound
Do you not hear the sound of music?
It calls out to you
Why won't you dance?

Sway your hips, tap your foot, wave your arms, bob your head
Why won't you free yourself?
Allow yokes to be broken and heavy burdens lifted
Lift up your head
Listen to the music
Why won't you dance?

The beat gives you reason to be free
Yet, you are just sitting there
You chose captivity over liberty
When life gets tough
The music becomes an outlet
Yet, you refuse to plug yourself in
Allowing no electrical charge to flow through your body
So you're dead
All your hopes and dreams are too far ahead
And in comes discouragement
Pushing you back further and further
But wait, the music still plays
Here's your opportunity to change your ways
Why won't you dance?

Dierra Merritt @2005

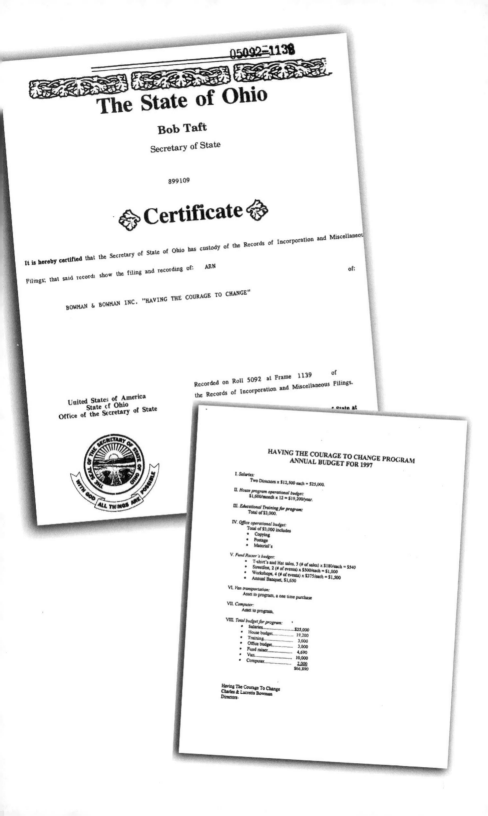

05092-1139

The State of Ohio

Bob Taft

Secretary of State

899109

❧ Certificate ❧

It is hereby certified that the Secretary of State of Ohio has custody of the Records of Incorporation and Miscellaneous Filings; that said records show the filing and recording of: ARN   of:

BOWMAN & BOWMAN INC. "HAVING THE COURAGE TO CHANGE"

Recorded on Roll 5092 at Frame 1139 of the Records of Incorporation and Miscellaneous Filings.

United States of America
State of Ohio
Office of the Secretary of State

HAVING THE COURAGE TO CHANGE PROGRAM
ANNUAL BUDGET FOR 1997

I. *Salaries:*
Two Directors x $12,500 each = $25,000.

II. *House program operational budget:*
$1,600/month x 12 = $19,200/year.

III. *Educational Training for program:*
Total of $3,000.

IV. *Office operational budget:*
Total of $3,000 includes
* Copying
* Postage
* Material's

V. *Fund Raiser's budget:*
* T-shirt's and Hat sales, 3 (# of sales) x $180/each = $540
* Sweeties, 2 (# of events) x $500/each = $1,000
* Workshops, 4 (# of events) x $375/each = $1,500
* Annual Banquet, $1,650

VI. *Van transportation:*
Asset to program, a one time purchase

VII. *Computer:*
Asset to program.

VIII. *Total budget for program:*
* Salaries............................$25,000
* House budget....................19,200
* Training..............................3,000
* Office budget.......................3,000
* Fund raiser..........................4,690
* Van...................................10,000
* Computer.............................2,000
  $66,890

Having The Courage To Change
Charles & Lucretia Bowman
Directors.

Section Three:

Ministry Model

>–I–‹›–O–‹›–I–‹

Program puts broken lives back together

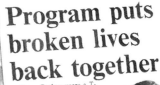

ALLEN HOWARD
NEIGHBORHOODS

Karen Booker wears a T-shirt that reads: "I am somewhere in the future . . . And I look much better than I look now."

She recites the quotation frequently because it keeps her from remembering a dismal past lifestyle that led to drug and alcohol addiction.

Ms. Booker is among a group of women who will graduate today from the Eve House in Evanston. She is part of the program Having the Courage to Change which operates the Eve House as an outreach ministry of the Christ Emmanuel Church in Walnut Hills.

The graduation ceremony will be from 6-10 p.m. at the Christ Emmanuel Ambassador Center, 1055 Laidlaw Ave., Bond Hill.

It took Ms. Booker 33 years to become optimistic about her future.

She said things started going downhill for her about age 13. It started with sex abuse by a family member, then came sex by friends she thought loved her. Before she knew it, she was drinking liquor and smoking marijuana practically every day.

Then along came crack cocaine. "I didn't intend to get hooked on crack, but before I knew I was," she said.

The next downhill spiral was to run away from home and drop out of school. The streets became a haven and another place to hide.

Nothing around her had any meaning. A relationship, a drink, a sniff of crack cocaine all fit into the life pattern she used to hold off pain.

(Please see HOWARD, Page B4)

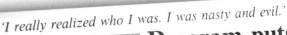

The Cincinnati Enquirer/Elisabeth Heimlich

Lucretia Bowman, who helps operate Eve House with her husband Charles, guided Karen Booker, right, in coping with her substance abuse.

Chapter Twelve

Teaching others through my experiences

I have been challenged to duplicate myself, and the ministry of *Having The Courage To Change.* I have been told (by my mentors, associates, and friends) that the work must go further, that I should begin to document what I do, and train capable people to complete a nationwide work. When I began the journey of writing this book I had several discussions about its focus, audience and intent, including whether or not it should be offered as an autobiography or an instruction manual. I decided to do a little of both with the hope that those who desire further information will contact me to receive it.

I consider myself to have learned and to understand much of my own process thus far. I even grasp a good deal of what it takes to operate a God-centered, social service organization; but I know I do not have all of the answers. I am still amazed at the transitions that have taken place in my own

*Everyone is not cut out for the work that I do and that's all right. My main focus in sharing my story with you was to help **you** to have the courage to change **your own life.***

life and how God has allowed and even destined me to affect the lives of others. Because of my personality and the way God made me, I have been able to do some things by God's grace and with sheer grit and discipline. I had to be free! I wasn't going to let any obstacle stop me. Discipline, combined with the ability to manage and lead, has caused me to successfully pour into others what I, through divine providence, had to learn on my own.

You impact the lives of others primarily by your own private success. You might be called to encourage one younger or older person along their path to recovery. Or, you could simply pass along a copy of this book to someone who needs it.

Some of you will be called upon to lead others to freedom. You, like a Sojourner Truth or Harriet Tubman, will not be content to bask alone in your freedom. You will have a burning passion for the freedom of others and you will be equipped to lead them into their individual lands of promise. I am writing this portion of the book to every Moses and Joseph of this generation. Those who are willing to abandon their former lifestyles to see others freed; those who are willing to be forerunners and trailblazers to lead people out of bondage! You feel a burning desire to help women or men, the elderly or youths, the addicted or abused, the disenfranchised, the poor, the educated but ignorant, those with bound creativity – any who need the courage to change!

Though the following list of *"To Do's"* is by no means exhaustive, there are a few things that I recommend for those intending to start work of this type:

Know Yourself

Know your strengths and weaknesses. Are you a people person? Do you handle money well? Are you a great administrator? Are you a good teacher or trainer? Do you have life experience that will help others? **What do you bring to the table that makes you able to start a program such as this?** What are your weaknesses, the areas with which you need assistance?

Don't let your inadequacies weigh you down – just get help where you need it. **The only limitations you have are those in your own mind.** Understand that you will probably not excel in everything; just do what you know to do, and do it well.

Let Others Assist You

It is vital in an endeavor such as this that you **begin to develop a team.** You may need to ask your accountant and/or lawyer friends to assist you with books or paperwork. I have a friend who has been my administrative assistant for years and initially volunteered to do all of my typing and paperwork. Eventually, I was able to put her on staff. She has even assisted with the writing of this book.

When I wanted to write my autobiography I asked for help because I am not a writer by trade. I have enlisted funding sources, a writer, editors, a graphic artist, — all people who believe in my story and were willing to see this vision come to pass.

Solicit The Support of Your Family

Family support is optimal and usually very helpful. The time and commitment it takes to develop and maintain a program like *Having The Courage To Change* is at times overwhelming. It is often spiritually, mentally, and emotionally challenging. It is sometimes dangerous. To have the understanding and support of your family will help to undergird your process.

If you cannot obtain this support, you will need to have a level of maturity so you won't feel hindered if you don't get support from your loved ones. At times, our loved ones do not understand or identify with our passion. We may have to lovingly (not defiantly) pursue that passion without allowing it to devastate our family relationships.

Do Your Research

Take the time to look into every aspect of what it takes to begin this type of ministry or program. Go to agencies, check the library, go on the Internet, talk to individuals, do whatever it takes to become knowledgeable about your process. For instance...

When you choose the location of the house, you'll also have to decide whether you will purchase the house outright or lease it. The location could present temptation or distraction to those who desire change, so you might avoid certain neighborhoods. The potential registration of former sex offenders may also be of concern to the neighborhood council.

Check the code requirements. Example: you must have a Fire Safety Inspection and an Insurance Inspection. This should be done before purchasing the home because there must be adequate square feet in each bedroom to qualify.

My husband and I lived on the top floor of the first house we used for *Having The Courage To Change*. This became a family issue because there really was no separation between "work" and "home." My husband was the only male in a home full of women.

Things like the above-mentioned items will bite you if you have not thought them through. You won't be able to avoid every obstacle. Many issues will surface by trial and error, but it is best to be as thorough as you can be.

Find a Mentor/Accountability Partner

Be accountable to someone regarding your vision. I submitted myself to the leadership of my local church, which helped me to stay focused and on course.

Experts often advise that you find someone in your field of interest who has already done what you're intending to accomplish. I have written this book with the goal of becoming a resource for those who wish to follow in my footsteps. There are social service programs in every city. They may not be formulated exactly like yours will be, but there is something you can learn from almost anyone in this field (social workers, judges, parole officers, etc.).

Make Sure You Follow Legal and Governmental Guidelines

For instance, become incorporated. This is a relatively simple step – you just fill out and send papers to the State government.

Be aware of zoning issues when having a "group" type home in the neighborhood. The neighborhood council must be notified of your intended activities.

Decide if you will be a *"Group Home"* or a *"Family Adjustment."* A Family Adjustment allows for five, unrelated people to live in a home whereas a group home has many more legal issues to consider.

There are many, many laws and guidelines to operating a program such as this. Make sure that you are apprised of them and maintain integrity and compliance with them.

Gather Funding

Fund your home by partners and donors. I have never accepted any government money; therefore, I don't have limitations on what I can do. Government money and, at times even private grant money, can put stipulations on you that are not a part of your vision. You need consistent givers who are aligned with you, with what you're doing, and how you're going about it.

Don't operate solely by monetary funds; investigate in-kind donations, estate trusts, and other types of funding that will perpetuate your vision — beyond your lifetime if necessary.

Foster Relationships By Networking

To build relationships, you will likely have to move outside of your circle of influence. You can start with friends and family, but they may not be able or willing to fund your program, make sure that it operates, or puts you in touch with the right people. If you are not a "people-person," this process will be particularly difficult for you, but your passion to see the vision accomplished will allow for the courage to change!

In this type of non-profit sector, there are many agencies that will provide or swap services. You have to get out there to see what is available. Someone may provide furniture for halfway houses. Another group may offer mentors for your participants. Some agencies will donate food or clothing. You have to know who they are, and they must know you as a trustworthy person with whom to collaborate.

Operate On A Budget

It has been said that a budget is a guide, not a god, but **you must be a good financial steward.** Develop an operating budget, but be ready to be flexible. In programs such as this, changes occur regularly. Your budget is what it takes to support you and those who will be served in the program. Your salary, daily food, clothing, housing, utilities, repairs, transportation, recreational activities, training materials, etc., should all be a part of the budget. Start where you are and build. The operating budget for my first house was about $150,000. Now it is over half a million for four houses.

Operate By Your Budget

You will have to account for it to the IRS, to the State, and to your donors. Your goal is to continue the work well beyond its first year. Most businesses take at least 3-5 years to become stable and make a profit. The ministry or program you are developing will take time to become an established success. You must be trustworthy for others to invest in you and your vision. Many times people don't invest in the vision: they invest in the *visionary*!

Be Willing To Work Hard and Do It!

Many a dream has been deferred or now lies in the graveyard because the person wanted to, even talked about it, yet *NEVER DID IT!* I suggest you set time aside now, while you're passionately reading this book, to get your vision on *PAPER*. Write it down! Only 5% of the population see their dreams accomplished. The common denominator of that 5% is that they have *WRITTEN DOWN* their goals!

Remember when you went to the grocery store with your list? You checked off every item and forgot none. When you went without your list, inevitably you forgot something or got too much of something else. **Your vision, mission and goals statement is the "TO DO LIST" for your LIFE!** Get it down and check off your items as they are accomplished. Do it not only for this particular dream, but your dreams for your family, your retirement, travel or any other thing you would like to see come to pass.

You will see Divine Providence meet you when write down and begin to act on your goals, visions, and dreams!

CONVICTION RECORD TRANSCRIPT
CITY OF CINCINNATI AND COUNTY OF HAMILTON

03-16-99

BY: LM

STATUS: NO CRIMINAL RECORD & NO TRAFFIC RECORD

SOCSEC:

NAME: BOWMAN, LUCRETIA A

SEX: F   RACE: B

DOB: 09-12-60

- -

<<< NO RECORD ON FILE >>>

Y

Chapter Thirteen

Obstacles to overcome

I was asked, *"What were the three greatest obstacles in starting Having The Courage To Change?"* I thought that was an interesting question, because I had already experienced so many obstacles in life, the ones I encountered starting the ministry were almost a cake-walk. This is an important point, particularly for those who have endured tragic situations but are STILL HERE! You've already endured more than your next obstacle will present; so you CAN DO IT! These three obstacles were the most pressing:

Nay-Sayers
I'd caution you to *be very selective about whom you give the privilege of sharing information about your dreams and visions.* Initially you will be very excited, others may not share in this excitement. Some may be dream-killers; they live in their own depression over things they have not done, or things that may have gone wrong, so they have no shortage of negative things to say to you. Others may be jealous of your achievements or even of your chutzpah. If you succeed, that sheds a poor light on them, and they will make opportunities to be critical.

You must be confident in what you are called to do. If no one but God stands with you, that's ok, and certainly more than enough. If people are going to feed you garbage, send them back to the dump where they belong! Get nurturing, positive people around you, those who want you to succeed and are willing to speak life to your plans. This is not to say that you do not accept or even expect *con*structive criticism or wisdom from those you trust — just not *de*structive trash-talking!

The Unwilling and Disobedient

There were people who knew they were supposed to help me, but did not. At times they would volunteer to do things and not follow through. On other occasions I would know that a particular need would be best served by this individual and I would approach them with it. There was an individual I believed should be working in the house with the women. The individual agreed but never got up the courage to make the life change and leave their area of comfort. People don't realize that their disobedience can cause a domino effect in the lives of those around them.

Learning To Wait On God

I would add to that, you must discern the right time to make life-changing decisions regarding the ministry. It is one thing (and at times a very difficult thing) to make life-changes that affect you and your family; it is another thing to have the lives of others in your hands. Of course, I know that we are all in God's hands, but He has entrusted me to help to shepherd the flock, under His care. You always want to make the right or best decision. I recommend that if you do not know what to do, STAND STILL AND WAIT. Don't make hasty or rash decisions, and allow PEACE to be your umpire. If you have no peace — don't do it!

I am often asked, *"How did you get to be so open?"* You see, I began by giving my testimony openly for everyone to hear. This includes my time of incarceration, the mental hospital and lesbianism – all topics that make people uncomfortable, and have caused many to live in shame and bondage for all of their adult life. *But my testimony opens doors for me, and sharing it actually frees me!* I am a transparent person: what you see is what you get. What you see is who I am. An enemy cannot attack me about my life because I have no hidden agenda; I am totally free! I don't worry about people saying, *"You know she was a thief and a lesbian, she's even been to jail!"* It's no secret. I'll tell you myself! *I'll also tell you how Christ delivered me and changed my life completely!* This makes those who are hurting open up to me, and allows the light in me to get to them. The same energy that I used to con people has evolved into a life-giving source of help, assisting those I encounter to be free — *if they choose to be.*

I HAVE NO FEAR OF WHO I AM OR OF WHAT I DID.
I know that everything I've done in my life has not been perfect. I also know that even now I am still growing, changing, making mistakes, and learning from them. The platform of my life and ministry is to face fear and change. You cannot just say your motto; you must live it!

Some advice:

Always Remain Teachable!
There is not a person on earth who has it all together. Everyone is more knowledgeable about his own story than the next guy. It is important that you be willing to learn from anyone. My participants have been homeless, drug-addicted, abused and neglected — people who many would not hear or even entertain — but I have learned so much from them. I learn from my husband, I learn from my son, I learn from my pastors and friends. Be a lifetime learner. *Humble yourself; you don't know it all!*

Often people ask me what type of person it takes to start this type of work. I am a firm believer that God can use anyone who is willing. But, I do know that...

YOU WON'T BE ABLE TO START A PROGRAM LIKE THIS IF...

You Are A Hypocrite
People are watching you, especially those with a history of criminal or other types of addictive behavior. They know a con when they see

one and they know genuineness when they see it. If you don't walk what you are teaching/preaching, you will not be successful in helping to change lives – because your life is not changed yet.

You Allow Phony and Superficial Relationships To Hinder You

Everyone does not have your best interest at heart. Everyone is not genuine, even in the non-profit or ministry sector. Everyone has not been willing to be processed or be changed. Some people have lived all of their lives being phony; it's all they've known. It's their means of survival.

There are times when I can't even be around certain individuals for long because there is such a stark difference in how we handle situations. Usually, they are equally as uncomfortable with me. When you encounter people who are not genuine, you cannot allow your disappointment to become a distraction from the work.

It has been said that people are in your life for a reason, a season or a lifetime. You must discern why that person is in your life. Are they a help or a distraction? Are they out for your best interest? Are they only there to do a project for a certain period of time or will you be bosom buddies for life? If you have proper expectations of your relationships, that will cut down on your disappointment!

The next question is, *"What causes ministries of this kind to 'hit or miss'?"* To this I reply...

It's Not Only Your Life Experience, It's Your Heart That Matters!

You must have a heart for the people you are helping. If you are genuine, they will recognize it, and they will open up to you. If you are not, you will just go through the motions and not see any effective change.

People Who Know They Are Loved Don't Have A Problem Submitting!

As the adage goes, people don't care how much you know until they know how much you care! Most non-profit and social service agencies don't have a money or resource problem, they have a LOVE problem. This is why they are so concerned with being conned or having altercations with their participants.

Most people are looking for that one person who will love them unconditionally, in truth, and with strength that is sometimes tough. These qualities go a long way. This is why many gangs are successful – the members feel like family. People need to have that same camaraderie when they travel on the journey to recovery.

You Must Be A Trustworthy Person - Especially With Money!

When former addicts began to give me $3,000 or $4,000 to keep for them, I knew they trusted me! When donors render goods, services, money and resources, I know they trust me, too!

I happen to be an extremely responsible person as it pertains to money; I believe this is part of why God has blessed me so much. If you are faithful with little, you will be trusted with much. I am very cautious about where and how my money is spent and invested, and I treat the finances of this ministry and of those who are affected by it with the same prayerful consideration. If you are faithful with what belongs to another, God will trust you with your own.

The Bible says that the love of money is the root of all kinds of evil. I have found that to be true in my own life and in the testimonies of many of my participants. It also says that the lust for money will cause much sorrow in your life. *Handling money is truly a test of character!*

Guard Yourself From Burnout!

Sometimes *the hopelessness of the workers* at these agencies/ministries causes the help they were attempting to give to start to deteriorate. Dryness occurs. There is no life in the ministry/agency or its employees. I caution you to keep yourself uplifted and set boundaries between your life and work. Use self-help materials, exercise, meditate, pray, or get counseling to keep yourself fresh, alert, and ready for those whom you serve. You are there to shine light. Don't let the light that is in you fade out!

Having The Courage To Change was designed to help people to go to the next level. It's about more than just addressing drug addiction and other serious issues. *It's about each of us overcoming our everyday fears and shouldering the courage to change in all areas of our lives.* It's about growing up, maturing, and making quality decisions that no longer devastate us, but bring us the quality of life for which we were born! *It's about teaching us how to stop abusing ourselves.*

The Foundational Principles of Our Lives

We will treat others the way we desire to be treated.

We will allow others to have a different view, opinion or outlook on life without attaching it to ourselves.

We will be focused on our change,
while encouraging others to do the same.

Final Thoughts

I hope that after reading my book and applying its
principles you are looking at your life and reflecting on
areas that may need to change.

What I've come to know is that change is never ending,
and learning to embrace it is a difficult challenge.
But you have to flow with change or change will flow without you.
Be open to the process to solve problems in your life that don't
even exist yet by embracing change.

Embrace change to live free...

Lucreta Bowman

About the Authors

Lucreta Bowman gives motivational speaking the right twist by utilizing biblical principles and scripture to inspire audiences to have the courage to change! Sharing her personal testimony of how God took her from the jailhouse to His house and from destruction to reconstruction, Lucreta allows the power of God to work through her to transform lives.

Lucreta was placed in foster care at birth and did not meet her biological mother until she was an adult. She was victimized as a child, abused, placed in a mental hospital, and became a runaway. Believing she was invincible, that no one cared, and searching for love and acceptance, she turned to a life of drugs and crime. This destructive lifestyle led to her being banished from the state of Ohio and incarcerated in state prisons.

Through surrendering her life to Jesus Christ and learning to embrace the process of change, Lucreta became the founder and director *Having The Courage To Change Ministry*. The New Beginnings House, Eve House, and Ruth & Naomi House are holistic housing programs for women who desire to change after experiencing addiction, incarceration, abuse or other destructive situations.

Lucreta resides in Cincinnati with her husband, Charles, and their two sons.

To contact Lucreta Bowman:
1947 Auburn Ave.
Cincinnati, OH 45219
513-345-1082
lbowman@citygospelmission.com

M (Melissa) Sadell Bradley is a native of Philadelphia, PA. Marion Moody, a local public school teacher, adopted her at age 3. She is a graduate of Friends' Central School in Merion, PA and holds a Dual Degree in English and African-American Studies from the University of Pennsylvania.

After graduating, Sadell moved to Cincinnati to work at the Procter and Gamble Co. A call to service led her to become a ministry leader at Christ Emmanuel Christian Fellowship where she served for 14 years as Director of Teen Ministry, and then as Director, and eventually Pastor of the Music, Worship, Arts and Communications Departments. She taught art and music at the Christ Emmanuel Christian Academy, and was an Adjunct Music Professor at The College of Mt. Saint Joseph.

Sadell Bradley has been a teacher, motivational speaker, and workshop presenter in a variety of venues. She is the primary writer, musical composer and artist on "Creative Grace," a CD and book compilation of stirring musical and intellectual inspirations to be released in January, 2006.

Sadell and her husband, Sherman B. Bradley II, founded Creative Grace Productions, LLC, a company that creates, publishes and distributes products and services to inspire, motivate and instruct. Creative Grace Productions, LLC also assists creative artists to present their works in the marketplace. Sadell and Sherman reside in Cincinnati.

To contact M. Sadell Bradley:
Creative Grace Productions, LLC
P.O. Box 24482
Cincinnati OH 45224
513-476-0485
www.creativegrace.net
email: sbradley@creativegrace.net